CLEOPATRA

Borgo Press Books Edited & Translated by FRANK J. MORLOCK

Alcestis: A Play in Five Acts, by Philippe Quinault * *Anna Karenina: A Play in Five Acts*, by Edmond Guiraud, from Leo Tolstoy * *Anthony: A Play in Five Acts*, by Alexandre Dumas, Père * *Atys: A Play in Five Acts*, by Philippe Quinault * *The Boss Lady: A Play in Five Acts*, by Paul Féval, Père * *The Children of Captain Grant: A Play in Five Acts*, by Jules Verne & Adolphe d'Ennery * *Cleopatra: A Play in Five Acts*, by Victorien Sardou * *Crime and Punishment: A Play in Three Acts*, by Frank J. Morlock, from Fyodor Dostoyevsky * *Don Quixote: A Play in Three Acts*, by Victorien Sardou, from Miguel de Cervantes * *The Dream of a Summer Night: A Fantasy Play in Three Acts*, by Paul Meurice * *Falstaff: A Play in Four Acts*, by William Shakespeare, John Dennis, William Kendrick, & Frank J. Morlock * *The Idiot: A Play in Three Acts*, by Frank J. Morlock, from Fyodor Dostoyevsky * *Isis: A Play in Five Acts*, by Philippe Quinault * *Jesus of Nazareth: A Play in Three Acts*, by Paul Demasy * *The Jew of Venice: A Play in Five Acts*, by Ferdinand Dugué * *Joan of Arc: A Play in Five Acts*, by Charles Desnoyer * *The Lily of the Valley: A Play in Five Acts*, by Théodore Barrière & Arthur de Beauplan, from Honoré de Balzac * *Lord Byron in Venice: A Play in Three Acts*, by Jacques Ancelot * *Louis XIV and the Affair of the Poisons: A Play in Five Acts*, by Victorien Sardou * *The Man Who Saw the Devil: A Play in Two Acts*, by Gaston Leroux * *Mathias Sandorf: A Play in Three Acts*, by Jules Verne & William Busnach * *Michael Strogoff: A Play in Five Acts*, by Jules Verne & Adolphe d'Ennery * *Les Misérables: A Play in Two Acts*, by Victor Hugo, Paul Meurice, & Charles Victor Hugo * *Monte Cristo, Part One: A Play in Five Acts*, by Alexandre Dumas, Père * *Monte Cristo, Part Two: A Play in Five Acts*, by Alexandre Dumas, Père * *Monte Cristo, Part Three: A Play in Five Acts*, by Alexandre Dumas, Père * *Monte Cristo, Part Four: A Play in Five Acts*, by Alexandre Dumas, Père * *The Musketeers: A Play in Five Acts*, by Alexandre Dumas, Père * *The Mysteries of Paris: A Play in Five Acts*, by Eugène Sue & Prosper Dinaux * *Napoléon Bonaparte: A Play in Six Acts*, by Alexandre Dumas, Père * *Ninety-Three: A Play in Four Acts*, by Victor Hugo & Paul Meurice * *Notes from the Underground: A Play in Two Acts*, by Frank J. Morlock, from Fyodor Dostoyevsky * *Outrageous Women: Lady MacBeth and Other French Plays*, edited by Frank J. Morlock * *Peau de Chagrin: A Play in Five Acts*, by Louis Judicis, from Honoré de Balzac * *The Prisoner of the Bastille: A Play in Five Acts*, by Alexandre Dumas, Père * *A Raw Youth: A Play in Five Acts*, by Frank J. Morlock, from Fyodor Dostoyevsky * *Richard Darlington: A Play in Three Acts*, by Alexandre Dumas, Père * *The San Felice: A Play in Five Acts*, by Maurice Drack, from Alexander Dumas, Père * *Saul and David: A Play in Five Acts*, by Voltaire * *Shylock, the Merchant of Venice: A Play in Three Acts*, by Alfred de Vigny * *Socrates: A Play in Three Acts*, by Voltaire * *The Son of Porthos: A Play in Five Acts*, by Émile Blavet, from M. Paul Mahalin * *The Stendhal Hamlet Scenarios and Other Shakespearean Shorts from the French*, edited by Frank J. Morlock * *A Summer Night's Dream: A Play in Three Acts*, by Joseph-Bernard Rosier & Adolphe de Leuwen * *The Three Musketeers: A Play in Five Acts*, by Alexandre Dumas, Père * *Urbain Grandier and the Devils of Loudon: A Play in Four Acts*, by Alexandre Dumas, Père * *The Voyage Through the Impossible: A Play in Three Acts*, by Jules Verne & Adolphe d'Ennery * *The Whites and the Blues: A Play in Five Acts*, by Alexandre Dumas, Père * *William Shakespeare: A Play in Six Acts*, by Ferdinand Dugué

CLEOPATRA

A PLAY IN FIVE ACTS

by

Victorien Sardou

Translated and Adapted by Frank J. Morlock

THE BORGO PRESS

An Imprint of Wildside Press LLC

MMX

Copyright © 1994, 2010 by Frank J. Morlock

All rights reserved. No part of this book may be reproduced without the expressed written consent of the author. Professionals are warned that this material, being fully protected under the copyright laws of the United States of America, and all other countries of the Berne and Universal Copyright Convention, is subject to a royalty. All rights, including all forms of performance now existing or later invented, but not limited to professional, amateur, recording, motion picture, recitation, public reading, radio, television broadcasting, DVD, and Role Playing Games, and all rights of translation into foreign languages, are expressly reserved. Particular emphasis is placed on the question of readings, and all uses of these plays by educational institutions, permission for which must be secured in advance from the author's publisher, Wildside Press, 9710 Traville Gateway Dr. #234, Rockville, MD 20850 (phone 301-762-1305).

www.wildsidebooks.com

FIRST WILDSIDE EDITION

CONTENTS

Cast of Characters 7
Act I, Scene 1: Tarsus 8
Act II, Scene 2: Memphis 41
Act III, Scene 3: A Terrace in Memphis 76
Act IV, Scene 4: Actium 100
Act V, Scene 5: Alexandria 145
Act V, Scene 6: Alexandria 169
About the Editor 187

DEDICATION

To

CARMEN,

FOR DANCING ON MY BIRTHDAY

CAST OF CHARACTERS

ANTHONY
OCTAVIAN
KEPHREN
DEMETRIUS
THRYSEUS
DELLIUS
DERCETAS
MESSANGER
OLYMPUS
GOVERNOR
NOTABLE
MERCHANT
STREPSIADES
DIVINER
JUBA
SLAVE
AMOSIS
QUEEN CLEOPATRA
OCTAVIA
CHARMIAN
IRIS
EROS (travesty)

ACT I

Scene 1

Tarsus

To the right, obliquely, a large portico reached by two sets of steps, shut by a wall of polished marble whose columns have heads of winged bulls face to face. In the middle of the wall a large door. To the left, a monumental gate, and by this gate, Persian awnings. In the distance, between two winged bulls with human heads, the sight of the quay and the shores of Cydnus, decorated with cypresses and laurels. In the midst of this, on the heights, sits the town, half Persian, half-Greek, crowned by a forest of cedars.

Several Roman legionaries, armed with pikes on guard grimly around the tribunal, guarding all exits. An anxious crowd (women with long veils, Cilician sailors, Merchants dressed like satraps) wait mutely and mournfully in stunned postures. The Governor and a group of Notables wander, whispering with gestures of despair. A Centurion appears under the portico.

CENTURION (to the crowd)
Go! Disperse! (to soldiers) Move back these insolents or they will soon invade the portico.

(The soldiers push the intimidated crowd back.)

MERCHANT (low to Governor)
You see. The legionnaires of the Triumvir treat us like a conquered people.

NOTABLE (low)
Or as vanquished rebels!

GOVERNOR
Patience! Here is someone who will tell us the news we've been waiting for.

(A young Slave comes to the Governor, running.)

GOVERNOR (anxiously)
Well?

SLAVE
Still nothing!

GOVERNOR
Nothing?

SLAVE
Nothing! No more boats on the Cydnus than litter on the beach.

GOVERNOR
Return to your post, child, and if, before the sun has run half its course, you announce to me the arrival of this Queen, I take the gods to witness, that for your reward I will set you free. Go!

(The Slave runs into the distance.)

NOTABLE
A promise, Governor, you won't have to keep. Cleopatra will not come. Audacious and truly royal, when it's a question of leading us in revolt against Rome, now that we are vanquished and Mark Anthony is punishing the cities of Asia Minor before his Tribunal this

whole Province of Cilicia, Cleopatra turns woman. Told to come she declares, from afar she will be the first at the rendezvous and, having lost her wager, she will pay for it. She even announces that she is en route.

The truth is she's keeping herself prudently shut up in her Egypt. You others, people of Tarsus, will suffer the rage of the Triumvir, as have the citizens of Ephesus and Sardis! Deliver your money—prepare your heads for the victor's axes!

MERCHANT
Why did we listen to that woman? Wasn't it your duty as Governor of Tarsus to avoid this madness?

GOVERNOR
It wasn't folly then! We believed what Cleopatra told us at the beginning of the war. Well, why not? Brutus' dagger had done justice to Caesar. Octavian, torn from his school bench, was rushing to Rome to claim his inheritance. Anthony disputed it with him, strong in his success and glory in the Forum. Fulvia, Anthony's ambitious wife, was finding him allies all over Italy. Brutus and Cassius were running all over the world. And if we hadn't seized this occasion to shake off the yoke of the Romans which their discord favored, what wise man, what prophet, what auger had foreseen these times of misfortune? Anthony, Octavian, and Lepidus recoiled from a common danger and formed a triumvirate; their united fleets dispersing the combined fleet of Sextus Pompey and Cleopatra; the battle camp of Philippi became the tomb of Brutus and Cassius—the conquerors dividing the universe. Anthony master of Asia ran over it as conqueror, pillaging our cities, confiscating our wealth, doubling our taxes, and in several months making us sweat out gold under blows of the sword or the ax—twelve million drachmas.

NOTABLE
Please gods he'll be content with our money and not give our heads to the lictors.

GOVERNOR
The gods are not for the vanquished: Cleopatra alone can divert Anthony's rage.

NOTABLE
And Cleopatra isn't coming.

MERCHANT
It's no use to think of fleeing. The countryside is full of soldiers—all the gates of the city are under guard.

GOVERNOR
To flee is to admit guilt and condemn oneself.

MERCHANT
Speak lower! Here are familiars of the Triumvir coming from that direction!

CENTURION
Make way!

SOLDIERS
Make way!

(The plaza empties before the newcomers. Demetrius, Dercetas, and Dellius leave the palace and come down the steps.)

DERCETAS (to Centurion)
Juba, who are all these people here? Inhabitants of Tarsus?

CENTURION JUBA
And from all the province of Cilicia. Princes or Magi, merchants, or soldiers—what do I know?

DELLIUS
And all compromised in Brutus' revolt?

CENTURION JUBA
More or less—under that heading, cited to appear before the Triumvir's Tribunal. (distances himself)

DEMETRIUS
Let them be reassured! Mark Anthony won't be more severe to them than to the inhabitants of Antioch or Ephesus. Terrible on his arrival, he will strike terror at first, then soften quickly after their supplications. And, after having threatened them with the ax, he will double their taxes. That's all. He is neither vindictive nor cruel.

DELLIUS
I've seen him less easy too often—in the days of the proscriptions—as Cicero's shade will attest!

DEMETRIUS
Fine. That murder wasn't committed by Anthony, but, indeed, by that shrew, Fulvia. He cannot refuse a woman—not even his wife.

DERCETAS
Softly. Beware of indiscreet ears.

DEMETRIUS
The spies have nothing to do with me! I don't say anything, Anthony absent, that I have not said a hundred times to him in person. He knows very well he has no surer or franker friend than Demetrius.

DELLIUS
That's certain!

DERCETAS
Sometimes, he listens more readily to his flatterers than his friends.

DEMETRIUS
At certain times. For of which Anthony do you speak? I know two, at least, so different, one from the other than one has trouble to rec-

ognize the same man. One is the libertine who never counts on anything more than his amorous prowess—and who talks with actors and freedmen, an unruly free liver who places his pride in drinking more toasts than that crazy Lepidus, and who, just the other day, couldn't pay too much for the discovery of a new dish, making a gift to his cook of a house confiscated that night. The other is a solder, frugal and careful, as hard on himself as others, the first in the attack, the last to retreat, the idol of his legionnaires, who sleeps with his fist shut in the snow and whom I have seen on the evening of a battle supping gaily on raw raisins washed down with water drawn form a stream! And his whole life offers the same contrasts. Balancing ceaselessly his duties and his appetites, glory which attracts him, pleasure which enchains him, sleeping in debauchery, he swiftly awakens with the prowess of a hero. So well does he hold me poised in suspense between admiration and blame that I am never closer to despising him than at the very hour he forces me to admire him more and while deploring his faults I always find excuse for them, for after all, his virtues profit Rome and his vices only wrong himself.

DELLIUS
Right. But, shouldn't your friendship, know how to guard him against so many enemies who are jealous of him? One especially, whom I haven't named and who takes an arm against him for each new fault.

DEMETRIUS
Of whom are you speaking? Just yesterday, I reproached Anthony for this masquerade in Ephesus, which he entered, followed by his ordinary escort of jugglers, mimes, clowns, dancers and mountebanks. I said to him: "Can you be seen in public with such men? Is this the escort of Caesar's avenger, the Conqueror of Philippi?"

DERCETAS
And what did he reply?

DEMETRIUS
Bah, he said to me, laughing: "I will improve with age; let us play gaily with the youth that remains to us."

DERCETAS
Truly, the adolescent Octavian is already older than he is.

DEMETRIUS
Indeed, he's a young greybeard. Ah, he's not the one who will give place beside him for wine, good cheer and women. He frightens me, this young sage, with his icy eyes, his thin lips which never break into a smile.

DELLIUS
And, by the way, isn't it his old tutor who came to us this morning?

DERCETAS
Thryseus? Yes! There he is, down there, admiring the course of the Cydnus.

DEMETRIUS
Did Octavian send him?

DERCETAS
Not at all. He, indeed, came himself, a pretended victim of the ingratitude and avarice of his pupil.

DELLIUS
On that score, he is not alone, is he?

DEMETRIUS
And Antony has actually welcomed him?

DERCETAS
He has made him his secretary.

DEMETRIUS
There's a fine recruit, this pedagogue—and our secrets will be well guarded.

DERCETAS
What? Do you suspect him?

DEMETRIUS
I distrust all deserters.

DELLIUS
Thryseus is not the first who abandoned Caesar's nephew to attach himself to Anthony's fortune.

DEMETRIUS
No, but he's the first to denounce Octavian with so much bitterness. And, I don't like a servant who speaks so ill of his old master.

DELLIUS
What evil can he say that Octavian doesn't deserve? That he's a skinflint, envious, and timid? It's justice—and I see no reason for suspicion.

DEMETRIUS
Let's say I'm deceived—but I would prefer a better friend of Octavian than this.

DELLIUS
Quiet. Here he comes.

(Thryseus comes to them.)

THRYSEUS
Worthy Dellius, hail!

DELLIUS
Hail to you, Thryseus.

THRYSEUS
Demetrius, hail!

DEMETRIUS (dryly)
Hail.

(DEMETRIUS goes off with Dercetas.)

THRYSEUS (to Dellius)
Has Dercetas told you I am with you?

DELLIUS
I learned it with joy.

THRYSEUS
I had your esteem and, I hope, your friendship. But, I am here. Enlighten me, I beg you. Is it indeed you that Anthony sent to Cleopatra?

DELLIUS
It was I.

THRYSEUS
The Egyptian didn't play with the Triumvir and his Ambassador this time?

DELLIUS
In what way? Cleopatra said she was happy to appear before Mark Anthony.

THRYSEUS
She's unaware of the perils to which she is exposing herself.

DELLIUS
She didn't risk less by affronting Caesar the day he landed in Egypt. Him, too, she braved by going to Pompey. Add, too, that she was strictly guarded by King Ptolemy, her brother, who guilty of the

same wrongs, counted on gaining his pardon for them by delivering Cleopatra to the justice of Caesar. Captive and condemned in advance—what to do? Wait for death?

Cleopatra clung to life. With the aid of a young Egyptian named Kephren, she succeeded in escaping, announced to Caesar she was sending him a box full of jewels taken from the royal treasure, and begged him to accept them as a token of her submission. The box arrived; Caesar opened it, it was Cleopatra, half nude, lowering her large gazelle's eyes and shivering from fear? From love? Who can say. The next day, Caesar dethroned Ptolemy and proclaimed her Queen of Egypt.

THRYSEUS
I know it.

DELLIUS
And this was not the intoxication of a day. On his return to Rome, Caesar brought Cleopatra there with him, and but for disturbances in the streets would have married her. Today she is in the full flowering of her beauty. And, moreover, this beauty, radiant and triumphant, is it not at the result of a strange charm which she releases and intoxicates us with? Is this an African philter, trickery or magic? I don't know. Still, no one in vain receives the caress of her glow, the enchanting music of her voice, the voluptuous treachery of her beauty. Exquisite musician, accomplished dancer, she is a poet by turns, struggles wisely with philosophers, debates science with savants, and knows, suddenly, the gravity of a queen, and lets it succeed the mad gaiety of a child. All languages are familiar to her—and all masks. Artificial and clever, she will charm you with her candor, or soften you with her tears. Still, Thryseus, all these women are united in a single woman—all poisons concentrated in one. That's Cleopatra.

THRYSEUS
In short, you think Anthony will let himself be captivated, like Caesar, by this Helen of the Nile?

DELLIUS
I don't know (triumphantly) But, now's the time!

(Noise of the crowd.)

NOTABLE
Powerful gods! Is it Anthony already?

GOVERNOR
Yes, for here's the Praetor who walks before him.

MERCHANT
And no Cleopatra.

GOVERNOR
We are lost!

(ANTHONY enters, then Kephren. A long shivering signals the appearance of the Praetor. At his gesture, an imperial fanfare responds, while the ushers, interpreters, scribes, etc. take the seats prepared for them. Then the Lictors appear in short mantles, their fasces covered, cutting edges turned backwards. They come in the midst of a brusque silence, take their places around the Tribunal, preceding, by several steps, Mark Anthony, a man in the strength of his age. Behind his head, Legionnaires raise the golden eagles with wings extended which hold lightning in their talons. A group of tribunes, soldiers, and officers, among them Demetrius, Ahenobarbus, Publicola, Dercetas, Dellius, Thryseus, surround him. The Chief Tribute bearers Numidians and Parthians, close the march. The crowed prostrates itself, hands extended, men and women shivering the while.)

CROWD
Mercy! Mark Anthony! Mercy.

ANTHONY (harshly)
Silence, everyone! Bring the Governor.

(The Centurion Juba, who makes a sign to the Governor who detaches himself, trembling, from the crowd and comes towards the portico where Anthony is seated.)

ANTHONY
Well, Governor, where is this Queen of Egypt that you promised us?

GOVERNOR
Deign to still wait, Triumvir. She cannot be much later in appearance.

ANTHONY
And why hasn't she come already?

GOVERNOR (stammering)
Who knows, sublime Anthony? The sea—contrary winds. Deign to continue waiting, from pity.

ALL
Yes, master, deign to wait.

ANTHONY (coldly)
I will wait until this hourglass is full.

(ANTHONY turns to the hourglass on the table.)

GOVERNOR
Think!

ANTHONY
And not an instant longer! (to Dellius) Where is this Egyptian officer who is said to precede her?

DELLIUS
Here he is. Approach.

(A tall man comes from the crowd, bronzed body under a cuirass of gold, silk tunic, a large gold bracelet on his wrist. His belt is of emeralds. He is wearing sandals. A heavy black hair descends to his neck.)

ANTHONY
Who are you?

KEPHREN
My name is Kephren. I command the Archers of the Divine Cleopatra.

ANTHONY
And, where did you leave the Divine Cleopatra?

KEPHREN
In the isle of Cyprus, where she made portage. It's from there that she sent me in advance to tell you that she was going to put sail, and that she would be at the mouth of the Cydnus at the same time as you.

ANTHONY
Well, I'm here and she is not.

KEPHREN
I have nothing to add to what I told you.

ANTHONY
Well, I add this, Lictors. Surround this man! (the Lictors surround Kephren) When this hourglass is full, if the Divine Cleopatra isn't here, put him in chains until further notice. (the Lictors lead him off into the distance) As for the Governor and the Notables who are Roman citizens, they have the right to the axe.

GOVERNOR (frightened)
Noble Triumvir, for pity!

NOTABLE (on his knees)
Allow us to purchase our lives! Fix the price!

ANTHONY
You will pay just as well dead as alive. Better!

NOTABLE
Anthony! In the name of Hercules your ancestor! Remember, we never fought against you.

ANTHONY
Three-quarters of the pirates of Sextus Pompey are Cilician sailors.

NOTABLE
Don't confuse us with them!

ANTHONY
Who paid them, if not you?

NOTABLE
From constraint, Anthony, with swords at our throats. And do not doubt it. Recall our long devotion to the Roman side!

GOVERNOR
And to Caesar, your friend.

NOTABLE
We who asked that our city be called The City of Caesar.

ANTHONY
Yes, from the time Caesar was dictator, but from the day that Brutus and Cassius butchered him, you supported Brutus and Cassius.

NOTABLE
Say that this Cleopatra made us more than senseless.

ANTHONY
So—she's going to be judged—present or not! And all of you with her.

NOTABLE
Invincible Anthony.

ANTHONY (coming to his Tribunal)
Breaker of oaths!

GOVERNOR (who follows him prostrate)
This for a miserable Egyptian woman!

ANTHONY
Am I to be importuned even here?

(Anthony makes a sign to the lictors who push the supplicants back.)

NOTABLE (overwhelmed)
We are done for!

(A silence. Anthony takes his place. He speaks low to the officers who surround him.)

ANTHONY
So, what do you say of this woman? Her audacity, is it credible? I am the judge and I am waiting! Doesn't this Cleopatra know who I am? Is she trying to confound the Triumvirs? Does she take me for that drunk of a Lepidus or for the callow Octavian? Her soldiers, that I have so often dispersed, haven't they taught her my name? Must I go besiege her in Alexandria and erect my tribunal on the cinders of her palace?

DELLIUS
Don't believe that Cleopatra wishes to defy you. She promised me to come and she will come. I bring myself as guaranty. Also, for sure, she's en route. Kephren told you.

ANTHONY
Fine proof. The testimony of Kephren.

THRYSEUS
You remarked the way he spoke of her as "The Divine Cleopatra."

ANTHONY
The brute adores her, no doubt of that.

THRYSEUS
She enchants all those who approach her.

ANTHONY
Caesar often told me that.

THRYSEUS
And yet Octavian, who saw her, didn't find her especially beautiful.

ANTHONY (gaily)
Truly? But, are you quite sure, Thryseus, that your student, this funny Octavian, knows much about women?

THRYSEUS
Between us, I don't think so.

ANTHONY
As for me, until proof is forthcoming to the contrary, I hold Caesar's opinion, who said of her: "She is at once, Phryne, Aspasia, and Semiramis.

DEMETRIUS
That's saying a lot.

SECRETARY (to Anthony)
Triumvir, the hourglass is full.

(A movement of fright in the crowd.)

ANTHONY (on his feet, aloud)
The hourglass is full. I won't wait any longer. Cleopatra knew little in advance the price of braving Mark Anthony. Here then! (to Lictors) You, do what I told you to this Kephren. You, uncover your fasces and surround these men! (pointing to the Governor and the Notables)

(Sensation.)

GOVERNOR
Mark Anthony!

ALL (begging)
In the name of the gods.

ANTHONY
Silence! It is Rome's turn to speak.

(Anthony raises his hand. The trumpets sound. The Lictors prepare to obey. But, like an echo in the distance, can be heard flutes and lyres, supported by sistri and tympani.)

DELLIUS
Listen.

THRYSEUS
What is this?

ANTHONY
Who dares to reply in this way to Roman trumpets?

DERCETAS
Look! Down there, on the Cydnus.

(The crowd moves toward the quay. Long murmurs of approval.)

DELLIUS (to Lictors)
Wait!

THRYSEUS (coming to the gate)
Strange marvel!

(The Romans have followed the movement of the crowd under the portico. Anthony finds himself isolated in his chair.)

ANTHONY (angrily)
Well? Where are you running?

DELLIUS (looking to the right)
The bark coming up the river, whose prow is gold and whose sails are purple; it slides on the waves, escorted by a cortege of women.

THRYSEUS
Is it the ship of Isis, goddess of Egypt? Or of Venus who reigns in the nearby isle of Cyprus?

(The barge approaches and lands amidst murmurs of admiration from the crowd.)

DERCETAS
Look, Anthony, look!

ANTHONY (brusquely)
That's right; I see.

THRYSEUS
So, this woman seated on the poop who comes to us in perfumes and music?

KEPHREN
It is Queen Cleopatra.

(Kephren bows profoundly.)

THRYSEUS (turning to Anthony)
One must agree she is beautiful.

ANTHONY
Be it so! But very imprudent to dare such a triumphal entry.

(Supported by her servant Charmian, Cleopatra has put foot on land. She is dressed in a tunic of transparent linen held by an enameled belt. She has a gold cassock and a veil. Bracelets jingle at her wrists. She has multiple necklaces. Rings sparkle on each of her fingers. She holds a scepter in the form of a cross. Behind her, two huge Nubian slaves hold fans of ostrich feathers. She starts to enter the portico. The legionaries approach. She holds her scepter upright.)

CLEOPATRA (haughtily)
Let them make place for the Queen of Egypt!

ANTHONY (on his feet)
What is this?

(Cleopatra, who is descending, raises her eyes, meets Anthony's glance and stops.)

CLEOPATRA
Tell me, Governor. This man is not Mark Anthony?

GOVERNOR
It is he, gracious Sovereign. It's to him you must speak, for your well-being and ours.

CLEOPATRA (without breaking her gaze on Anthony)
And what shall I say to him? Do I even know what this Mark Anthony accuses me of?

ANTHONY (beside himself)
You don't know, you say?

CLEOPATRA
If I ever knew, I wouldn't forget it.

ANTHONY
What? Isn't it enough to be late in coming? Are you come to play with me?

CLEOPATRA (proudly)
Triumvir! I am Queen of Egypt. I indeed intend to reply to Rome's questions. But I will not take all these people as confidants for my answers.

ANTHONY
You prefer to speak without witnesses? So be it! Your cause won't get any better. Let them leave us and close the gates.

(They leave their seats and go towards the palace. The crowd goes toward the river. He speaks to the Lictors.)

ANTHONY
You will answer to me for Cleopatra's accomplices.

THRYSEUS (low to Dellius)
You hear him?

DELLIUS (low to Thryseus)
Yes.

THRYSEUS
And this man will dishonor himself for a smile.

DELLIUS
Right! The Egyptian has her sorcery.

(All the officers of Anthony, Cleopatra's suite, the Governor and the Notables leave the portico. The legionaries shut the gate. Outside, the crowd waits anxiously. Anthony, after having gone to the back, comes to Cleopatra who he finds, to his surprise, seated tranquilly on the cushions that her women have placed for her. After a gesture of scorn, he resumes.)

ANTHONY
Well? Now we are alone.

CLEOPATRA (pointing to a cushioned seat at some distance)
Deign to have a seat.

ANTHONY (brusquely)
And you, deign to listen to me! Since you pretend to forget of what Rome accuses you, I am going to remind you. (going and coming) "I don't remember," you say! Doubtless you've forgotten the first of your imprudent actions—which was to aid Pompey the Great against Caesar—nor the danger you were in of losing your crown and your life?

CLEOPATRA
As for the danger I was in—I don't recall it. As for Caesar, yes, surely I remember him.

ANTHONY
And of having steeped him with philters like a sorceress of Egypt, that you are, it seems.

CLEOPATRA
A sort of nourishment for Roman brats that threaten Cleopatra, when they are not wise.

ANTHONY
Do you say, that if you hadn't had recourse to magic, Caesar would have lingered so long in this love affair? Until he made you come to Rome, to the point of intending to make you his heir, and repudiating for you, his wife and marrying you—he, the dictator, you a barbarian!

Happily, Rome became indignant. Rome didn't permit Caesar to give this pretext to his murders. Rome sent you back to Egypt. And that's what you cannot forgive. Precipitated to the pinnacle where you sit enthroned, you swore to render to Romans affront for affront, and you have attempted to hasten your vengeance. Your fleet cannot accomplish the work you dream of? You address yourself to Sextus Pompey who puts his pirates in your service. You breathe your hate into all Asia Minor from the Delta to the Hellespont, and at the same time you aggrandize Alexandria, giving to a library already rich, that of Pergamum, you gather all the artists of Greece and the wise men of Chaldea, and you boost of creating a city to rival Rome, to oppose to the Republic an Empire of the East and thus to move the axis of the world. Do you still say this is an old wives' tale? A witness accuses you—that you cannot disavow. Yourself! I have quoted word for word your letter to Sextus Pompey. Here it is. (pointing to a papyrus on the table)

CLEOPATRA
Why shouldn't I write him, since I was his ally?

ANTHONY (ironically)
And, why wouldn't you be his ally, after having been his father's ally?

CLEOPATRA
If you yourself were being honest, this is not what you are really accusing me of.

ANTHONY (discomfited)
No, truly!

CLEOPATRA
Then, precisely, I beg you.

ANTHONY (coming to her)
Well, I accuse, since I must tell you, of being allied with Caesar's assassins.

CLEOPATRA (with a shout)
I? Immortal gods! I, who he wished to make his wife! I! Cleopatra! I would have linked my hand with their bloody frightful hands?

ANTHONY
They affirm it.

CLEOPATRA
Prove it, then! Prove me guilty of this infamy! And I will deliver myself to your lictors.

ANTHONY
Have you forgotten what you dared here? The day that the fleet of Octavian pursued Brutus and Cassius? Didn't you set sail expressly to bar his passage?

CLEOPATRA (forcefully)
That, yes. I did that.

ANTHONY (triumphant)
Ah! Again! And, you were not allied with Brutus and Cassius?

CLEOPATRA
If I had been, I would also have barred your passage, as you, also, were pursuing them. I would have tried it, at least, as Sextus Pompey attempted to do. I would have disputed your supreme victory at Philippi. I did not do it!

ANTHONY (surprised)
No, that's true. Why?

CLEOPATRA
Don't you understand? And, I am the enemy of Rome (lowering her voice) because I am the enemy of Octavian?

ANTHONY (who is reproaching himself)
You! What are you saying?

CLEOPATRA
Losing the love of the man who shook the world would not have bothered me so much had his inheritance fallen into your hands, nor accepting you for my master, you who were his bravest lieutenant, his best friend and his avenger. You are his equal and I seem to find him again in you.

ANTHONY (softened)
Well?

CLEOPATRA
From the Conqueror of the Gauls to the Conqueror of the Parthians is not a loss.

ANTHONY
So be it, but—

CLEOPATRA (without listening to him)
But, to submit to the law of this school boy with bad eyesight?

ANTHONY
I realize that Octavian is very young.

CLEOPATRA
If this imperious face doesn't mask the soul of an old man, cowardly an dried up, closed to all grand passions—

ANTHONY (with satisfaction)
Come, you exaggerate.

CLEOPATRA
Defend him! A man made to be a slave!

ANTHONY (softly)
Oh!

CLEOPATRA
Cruel after victory; cowardly during battle.

ANTHONY
Let him be as he chooses, you forget that Octavian—

CLEOPATRA
Yes, I would forget you expected to share with him and Lepidus, his straw-man, the realms you have conquered, you and Caesar, and but for the default of Caesar, you ought to have governed alone.

ANTHONY
What's signed is signed.

CLEOPATRA
Ah! Why am I not Anthony instead of Cleopatra?

ANTHONY
But, what? How could I go against Caesar's testament?

CLEOPATRA (ironic)
The one you read in the Forum? Right?

ANTHONY
Doubtless.

CLEOPATRA
A miserable scribbling, in which neither you nor I were mentioned? You believe such a will?

ANTHONY (sitting near her)
You question it?

CLEOPATRA (lowering her voice)
I don't question it. I am sure that a will which disinherited both of us wasn't Caesar's; it was Octavian's.

ANTHONY
Ah, if only I had proof!

CLEOPATRA (jesting)
You allow yourself to be taken in by his protestations of friendship?

ANTHONY
No, certainly not. I am quite sure that he hates me more—

CLEOPATRA
More than he hates me?

ANTHONY (familiar, seated by her)
Oh, you, for a long while, for the great passion you had inspired in Caesar, and his fear of seeing you inherit from his uncle. This hate goes so far as to question your beauty.

CLEOPATRA
Truly!

ANTHONY (gaily)
I guarantee you he's wrong! And that it deserves its fame.

CLEOPATRA
Alas! What has it gained me up to now but the furor of the Romans?

ANTHONY
But here, at least, it is good to plead its case and win it. Plato says that a harmonious face proves a soul is truly noble. If your transparent eyes do not reveal a loyal soul, it is a treason to the gods—as if the stars misled the sailors. Not just your words, your beauty justifies you and attests to me you are loyal to Rome.

CLEOPATRA
So long as Rome is Mark Anthony.

ANTHONY
It's well I understand you. Moreover, Octavian is alone in his opinion, and if the Romans detest you, it's for the love you inspire to all those who you permit near you like me.

CLEOPATRA (smiling)
And that have never inspired me with love for them, it must be admitted.

ANTHONY (struck)
None, you say?

CLEOPATRA (tranquilly)
None!

ANTHONY
You? Cleopatra, you've never loved?

CLEOPATRA (smiling)
Never.

ANTHONY
You are jesting?

CLEOPATRA (ingenuously)
Alas, no. But, what? Married very young to my brother Ptolemy, also young like me. I found nothing in this marriage but bitterness and disgust. Much later, dazzled by the fame of Caesar, I gave myself to him, carried away by enthusiasm in which the heart had no part. A day's error, expiated by cruel deceptions. So, you see, a child, an old man—that's all my life.

ANTHONY (incredulously)
And, no other?

CLEOPATRA (proudly)
And on what other would I have deigned to lower my glance? None being King, like Ptolemy, a half god, like Caesar.

ANTHONY
By Hercules! It's an injury to the gods that you take no profit from the prodigious gifts they've showered on you without measure.

CLEOPATRA (smiling sadly)
I do them this injury. And, perhaps, after all, it's better that it be so.

ANTHONY
Why?

CLEOPATRA
Ah, because whoever I would love well, this time I would love too much.

ANTHONY
Too much?

CLEOPATRA
For his misfortune and mine. For, first of all, I would be crazy, lost, madly jealous.

ANTHONY
Well?

CLEOPATRA
And despotic! Ah, that one, the one I might still love! He would have to be mine completely, without a look, a thought, a memory of another, as I would be everything to him, in the virginity of my soul and my feelings! I would have him sacrifice all the world to me: a husband, his wife, a father, his children, a son, his mother, a citizen, his country, as I would throw at his feet all virtue in the immodest pride of my love. And, triumphant in my fall, glorious in my shame, I would say to Egypt, to Rome, to the entire world: "Yes, I love him.

Yes, I am his. I, the Queen, I, Cleopatra, I am his slave!" And, if my people revolted, let Rome wax indignant and insult me. Let the universe take arms against me. Let heaven itself ready its lightning. I will not sacrifice a single one of our kisses to the clamor of men, to the rage of the gods.

ANTHONY (standing, like her, exalted)
That's wonderful! O woman, true woman, yes, it is thus one must love.

CLEOPATRA
Ah, I am not one of your Roman matrons, for whom love is only a domestic duty, whose only end is motherhood. Flowers without perfume, fruits without the savor of the Gynaeceum, hiding under triple wrapping their snowy and frozen bodies which they hardly dare to deliver themselves without veils to the caresses of their master. Daughter of Egypt and of Greece, I am of another race and the African sun which has tanned my face has put in my breasts other flames. Let the one comes who will give wings to the passion that runs in my soul and, failing nourishment, will devour it, and my flesh will embrace his flesh with the same fires, my blood will run with the same ardor in his veins! My arms will be on his shoulder like a tunic of Nessus on the flanks of his ancestor Hercules and this furious love must consume us both and reduce us to cinders, this will be my pride and my joy, to be burned by him, and my sensuality to die of it.

ANTHONY
By heaven! The one into whom you pour such intoxication will be the equal of the gods!

CLEOPATRA (with pretended confusion)
But truly, I am forgetting myself. (sits down) Let us leave these dreams and return to Rome.

ANTHONY (sitting closer to her)
Ah, sorceress! They weren't lying when they told me I could not brave with impunity the witchcraft of your lotus eyes and your caressing voice. I understand the infatuation of Caesar for the Egyptian, as they call you. And, I envy him for having loved you so much and I pity him for not knowing how to inspire you with a love equal to his! What man would not forget for you, mother, wife, children? And would not accept exile even from his country to find a more beautiful home in your heart?

CLEOPATRA
Yes, if he was my equal. He who, of all, is the first, will belong only to the first.

ANTHONY (avidly)
And if I were he?

CLEOPATRA
So be it!

ANTHONY
And you love?

CLEOPATRA (stopping him with a gesture)
Oh, let's speak of you first. It's enough that I permit it. Anthony is accustomed to quick victories. But Cleopatra is not disarmed so quickly.

ANTHONY
I swear to the gods and by the sudden passion which maddens me.

CLEOPATRA (joking lightly, playing to the crowd)
True! Since you already forget the people for it.

ANTHONY (calmly)
Those people there? It's true. I was forgetting them! Let's decide their fate. (rising) Juba! Open the gates.

(Cleopatra remains seated, nonchalant. All the people enter. Romans to the right. The others to the left and back. They are anxious, humble.)

ANTHONY (without looking at Cleopatra)
People of Tarsus and Cilicia, hear the decree of your judge. (scared, all shivering they fall to their knees. To Cleopatra in a low voice) What shall I say to them? What do you think about it? Must I treat them as rebels?

CLEOPATRA (tranquilly)
If they are guilty, so am I. Decide.

ANTHONY
Then, you order me to pardon them?

CLEOPATRA
Have I the right to order? I am hardly permitted to express a wish.

ANTHONY (tenderly)
Is it their pardon you desire?

CLEOPATRA (without looking at him)
Entirely.

ANTHONY
Without amends or confiscation?

CLEOPATRA
Unreserved.

ANTHONY (insisting on having her look)
You wish it?

CLEOPATRA (her eyes on his)
I beg you.

ANTHONY (aloud)
Rise! I grant you mercy.

(Acclamations of joy.)

CROWD
Sublime Anthony! Hero! Demi-god! Long life to the Triumvir! To Mark Anthony!

ANTHONY
Thank the Queen who has proved your innocence by proving hers.

(The crowd prostrates itself before Cleopatra.)

CROWD
O goddess! Illustrious Queen! O very precious.

ANTHONY
Go on, go on. That's enough. Now, leave us alone.

(With a gesture the lictors force the crowd off the stage. To Cleopatra, who has risen with the aid of her women, in a low voice.)

ANTHONY
Are you satisfied?

CLEOPATRA (tenderly)
Yes.

ANTHONY
And, you will be obliged to me for it?

CLEOPATRA
All my life.

ANTHONY
Deign to accept the hospitality that I offer.

CLEOPATRA
It is for me, the Queen, to offer you my roof and my table! Will you follow me?

ANTHONY
Wherever you are pleased to lead me! Even were death along the way. (makes a sign to Juba)

CLEOPATRA
Come, then.

(Juba makes the crowd go off. Flutes, tambourines, and sistri. Cleopatra and Anthony reach the boat and get ready to depart in the midst of acclamations.)

DELLIUS (jesting)
Well, then, Thryseus!

THRYSEUS
I have lost.

CURTAIN

ACT II

Scene 2

Memphis

A vast hall which prolongs an avenue of sphinxes with heads of sheep which descends to the Nile. To the right a door. A table is set against large columns covered with hieroglyphics supporting a cedar ceiling that permits sight of an immense blue heaven.

Anthony, stretched on cushions of red hair, dressed in an Egyptian robe, holds his cup to the cup-bearer while Cleopatra strips the petals off roses. Now some clowns, with tall miters, jesting and grimacing, clashing cymbals. The officers of Anthony, in long tunics, watch, seated on folding chairs, mixed with Egyptian officers. Iris one of Cleopatra's servants thinks, standing by a column.

ANTHONY
Enough of those clowns! Don't we have a snake charmer?

CLEOPATRA
No, no. No serpents. But, rather my Nubian dancers. Let them be called!

(The dancers enter.)

ANTHONY
More reptiles if we were to judge by the suppleness of their figures.

CLEOPATRA
The undulations of their bodies are more agreeable to see, you will agree, than those of your serpents of the Nile.

ANTHONY
Yes, indeed! Come, my beauties, rejoice our eyes and charm our ears.

(Music and dances. After a while Charmian comes in from the right and calls to Iris in a low voice.)

CHARMIAN
Iris!

(Iris doesn't hear her. Charmian goes to her.)

CHARMIAN
Iris!

IRIS (leaving her thoughts)
You are calling me?

CHARMIAN
Always melancholy? What are you dreaming about, that beautiful Kephren?

IRIS (confused)
Me?

CHARMIAN
Who doesn't even think of looking at you?

IRIS
Alas!

CHARMIAN
Ah! How wrong you are! Ah! How mad I am at you for crying over that man!

IRIS
Where did you see me crying?

CHARMIAN
In your eyes. But, come aside. I have something here to make you laugh.

(Charmian pulls Iris aside.)

IRIS
What is it?

CHARMIAN
You know, this Thryseus, who used to be Octavian's tutor, and is now Anthony's secretary?

IRIS
Well?

CHARMIAN
I was right. He is in love with me!

IRIS
Him?

CHARMIAN
Him.

IRIS
Say that he knows you are very talkative and very particular and that he finds listening to you pleasant and profitable.

CHARMIAN
And, I tell you, he loves me.

IRIS
And he told you so?

CHARMIAN
Never! He doesn't dare, the poor pedagogue! But, what he doesn't say to me, he confides to his notebooks. He never leaves me without scratching something in them.

IRIS
Truly! All that he told you!

CHARMIAN (without listening to her)
Just now, I surprised him, his notebooks in his hands. And, seeing me, he quickly slid them in his belt, so quickly that they fell. He was so concerned that he did not see it. Here they are.

IRIS
You kept them?

CHARMIAN
Let's bet they are verses. (opens them) And full of me!

IRIS
That's what you want.

CHARMIAN
To convince you. (reads while the music and the dancing continues) "Alexandria. More than ever Dellius' predictions are fulfilled. Since we've come to Egypt, the love of the Triumvir for the Queen passes all belief and seems like madness."

IRIS
Much lower! Take care, he might hear you.

CHARMIAN
Good! It is all about her—as she is all about him. (starts reading again) "Today, the third day of the month of Athyr, the fourth of rising of the Nile after having bestowed on the Queen the honors of a triumph over the people he conquered, Anthony publicly gave her a gift of the realms of Cilicia, Syria, Phoenicia, Arabia, and Judea. This same evening, to better prove that he has broken off all commerce with Rome, he tore up a letter from Fulvia without reading."

IRIS
In all this, there's no question of you.

CHARMIAN
Nothing at all, yet! Let's go further. (turns the pages and reads) "The fifteenth day of the same month, feast of the new moon. Anthony wants to leave Egypt. Cleopatra won't let him. That's how she has caught herself—she, too, she loves him to distraction. She doesn't see or listen anyone except to him, anticipates all his desires, lends herself to all his caprices. To night, Anthony had the fantasy of disguising himself as a sailor and to make the Queen dress in the clothes of a young boy. In this outfit they ran, by the light of the moon, through the streets of Alexandria, knocking on doors, shouting 'Fire!' to terrify the good sleeping burghers. One of those whose verger was pillaged, being left with his slaves, would have beaten soundly the conqueror of the Philippi and the Divine Cleopatra before they were known, if Kephren had not arrived to protect them. The Queen who adores these nocturnal expeditions was ravished by this which she laughed at still in the morning at her toilette as Charmian told me!"

IRIS
Ah! Finally!

CHARMIAN
There I am.

IRIS
And, then?

CHARMIAN
And, then? (looking) That's all.

IRIS
About you? Nothing more?

CHARMIAN
Nothing!

IRIS
Well, there's a love that will never waste away.

CHARMIAN
Oh, the monster!

IRIS
Give me.

(Iris takes the notebooks.)

CHARMIAN
Look at what he wrote just now.

IRIS
Shall I go on to the end then?

CHARMIAN
Yes.

IRIS (reading)
"Third day of the harvest. Since yesterday we've been at Memphis, after having gone up the Nile and visited the pyramids, stayed in an old palace of the ancient Pharos and abandoned since Cambyses and very badly lodged it must be said."

CHARMIAN
Ah, yes!

IRIS (reading)
"But love and pleasure lose nothing and if I believe the precious Charmian—"

CHARMIAN
Here we go!

IRIS
"Who chatters like a magpie—"

CHARMIAN (revolted)
Oh!

IRIS
Hush! Here he is.

(Iris closes and hides the notebook.)

THRYSEUS (to himself, preoccupied, looking at the ground)
How could I have been so stupid? Happily, the notes are unsigned. No matter! If they fall into the hands of Cleopatra.

CHARMIAN
You've lost something, Thryseus?

THRYSEUS
Me?

CHARMIAN
Your notebooks, perhaps?

THRYSEUS
What?

CHARMIAN (without giving them to him)
Here they are.

THRYSEUS
Ah, you found them?

CHARMIAN
On the terrace.

THRYSEUS
Ah?

CHARMIAN (returning the notebooks to him)
But, relax. I haven't read them.

THRYSEUS
Oh, you could. You would have seen the outlines of a history of Anthony and Cleopatra that I propose to write.

CHARMIAN
Really?

THRYSEUS
And, of which you could boast of having furnished me the best part.

CHARMIAN
Me?

THRYSEUS (tenderly)
In deigning sometimes to do me the honor of talking with me.

CHARMIAN
Like a magpie!

(Charmian goes off with Iris.)

THRYSEUS (alone, hugging the notebooks)
She did read it!

CLEOPATRA (to Anthony)
Ah! Here's Kephren. Well? Those lions? What news?

KEPHREN
Such as you wish them, light of the world!

CLEOPATRA (ravished)
Ah! Let's see that.

KEPHREN
Every evening, a lion with a nice figure, a lioness and her cubs come to drink at the sacred pool of the Ptah, near the gate of the white wall.

CLEOPATRA
At what time?

KEPHREN
At the hour the first stars open their golden eyes.

CLEOPATRA
And, how many lion cubs?

KEPHREN
Two. I have watched their tracks.

CLEOPATRA
I want to take them alive. The ships are ready?

(They rise and come down.)

KEPHREN
Yes, mistress, and the bows and spears. But, there's no need to leave right away, and you cannot take a hiding place until the sun is on the horizon.

CLEOPATRA
Without doubt. Let us let the heat of the day ease. But alive! You understand?

KEPHREN
I will bring them to you myself, like two dogs.

CLEOPATRA
Do it, Kephren, and what you want—ask for it.

KEPHREN
Permit me, during this hunt, to stay by your side.

CLEOPATRA
Are you forgetting that Mark Anthony is there to defend me?

KEPHREN
No, truly!

CLEOPATRA
Oh, do you fear he won't be enough?

KEPHREN
I have the right to fear everything when your life is in question.

CLEOPATRA (standing)
You say?

ANTHONY
He's right.

CLEOPATRA
What?

ANTHONY (on his feet)
No anger, come. Don't let him leave this way. Give him the blessing of a smile.

CLEOPATRA
No, certainly not. When he dares to displease me.

ANTHONY
Poor Kephren! Have you the courage to stay angry with him?

CLEOPATRA
Are you going to plead for him?

ANTHONY
What do you want? I pity him.

THRYSEUS (who has approached)
He's not to be pitied.

CLEOPATRA
Why's that?

THRYSEUS
Isn't it a joy sufficient, being loved?

ANTHONY (gaily)
It's not a joy sufficient for me.

CLEOPATRA
It's still necessary that they love you?

ANTHONY
Yes!

CLEOPATRA
And, loved by who?

ANTHONY
You.

CLEOPATRA
Then, you are happy?

ANTHONY
More than a mortal can be.

CLEOPATRA
Yes, right?

ANTHONY
Here, especially. Certainly. Alexandria is beautiful with its school and its museums and boats running to the light of Pharos like butterflies to the flame of a lamp. But, what? Under its marble porticoes, before its temples like to the Parthenon, I could still believe in Greece. Here, at Memphis, in face of the desert, I feel, indeed, in your realm. Here, your beauty appears to me more foreign, in the shadows of these forests of granite or in the blazing clarity of these burning horizons. I see it better in you, the daughter, the flower of this silent Egypt where everything is symbolic and mysterious, even the language of your priests, even the victory songs graven on these columns, here, still, more than before with your profound eyes, your enigmatic smile and your snakelike suppleness, you are, indeed, truly the Egyptian, the Isis always veiled in shadows, the living enigma, the sphinx.

CLEOPATRA
And, it's here that I love you with all my soul! Here that I do not live except by you, and through you, and here that I put all my pride in you. Here that I forget for you alone, all my projects of hate and domination which are not worth one of your smiles. Is it not surprising that I am come to that, from the depth of my proud heart to the

flame of yours? I, Queen, I, Cleopatra! And, without having wished it—in spite of myself.

ANTHONY
In spite of yourself?

CLEOPATRA
Surely, yes. I can admit, at present, you won't hold it against me. Down there, in Tarsus, I had only one idea—to seduce you like Caesar, and, in pretending love, to protect myself, to dominate you the more surely. (Anthony moves abruptly) Oh, I am telling you everything, you see, I am frank. But, I was taken in my trap. From the day of my easy victory, I saw you, so tender, so confiding, your virile charm, your valiant smile, your royal manners, have, indeed, conquered me. So that, quite softly, without taking precautions, this love which I thought was feigned, that I felt to be so good, and I judged it still to be a lie, when it had already become a truth, a great truth. The only truth is that I adore you. That you are my master, my King, and that I am, indeed, happy. Too much so, perhaps! I am afraid.

ANTHONY
Afraid?

CLEOPATRA
Yes, my joy is too great. It's the hour that the immortals are jealous of us and make us expiate the joys they give us. At the point of happiness we've reached, there's nothing left to expect but disasters. I am afraid of the unknown, of the unexpected, of tomorrow.

ANTHONY
What an idea!

CLEOPATRA
And, besides, our life must expand through its entirety without hostile fortune, and without cares, each day bringing the same joys, each day is only a step towards the inevitable, age, and death! How-

ever great, however durable our love may be, the hour will come when my eyes will shine less to charm you, yours flame less to tell me of it, or my body will be less supple to entwine you and your heart less tender to support mine. And it is frightful to think of that, admit it! Oh, to die, suddenly in the full drunkenness of life, in the full sensuality of love. What a dream!

ANTHONY
The dream of all lovers.

CLEOPATRA
I think it, do you believe it, every day, every instant and never more than at the time I am in the greatest ecstasy in your arms. Ah, I wish that at that moment your life and mine were suspended on our lips, to be broken on a kiss.

ANTHONY
That, surely, would be an enviable death.

CLEOPATRA
You will have it, if it pleases you to share it with me. For a long while, I've wanted this ending on the day when fortune goes contrary, and I have asked it of the one man capable of assuring me of it. (to Charmian) Has Olympus come?

ANTHONY
What, your doctor? This sorcerer?

CLEOPATRA
Speak better of a man that the wisest listen to with respect. Olympus is a sage who lives far from people in a mysterious retreat, where he studies all the secrets of the earth, the same that my astrologer Satni finds in the heavens. For nothing escapes these men, neither the present nor the future. Isis raises all her veils to them. Satni predicts fortune, good or bad, and the very day I embarked from Alexandria to appear before you, do you know what he told mw?

ANTHONY
What did he say to you?

CLEOPATRA
"Queen, take care, your victory may not be a defeat."

ANTHONY
Indeed, there's my augur with his double menacing words.

CLEOPATRA
What? Wasn't it admirable, this prediction? And, victorious over Anthony, have I not been conquered by him?

ANTHONY (smiling)
Yes, surely. They can explain everything in this way.

(Olympus, an old man more like a priest than a doctor, approaches.)

CLEOPATRA
Come forward, Olympus! Have you obeyed your Queen?

(So saying, Cleopatra seats herself.)

OLYMPUS
Yes.

(Anthony is still on his feet.)

CLEOPATRA
And what I told you to look for? Have you found it?

OLYMPUS
The remedies which cure life are easier to discover than those which delay death. From the juice of dreaded plants I have composed a beverage whose effects I have tried on diseased animals and on the condemned. To make a cadaver of a live person two drops suffice. I have placed twenty drops in a slender container of amber which I

have given the aspect of a pearl. Here it is encased in this ring. The day when you wish to leave the light of men, dissolve this pearl in your cup and drink. In a glance, it will be the end of Cleopatra.

CLEOPATRA (taking the ring)
Fine, Olympus. But this poison—will it disfigure me? For that is important. I've told you; I wish to remain beautiful even after death. I want to leave an effigy in which the charm the gods have given me persists and survives. I want, on the day when sacrilegious soldiers open my sarcophagus and strip me of my bandages and lift my golden mask, I want my face to appear to them admirable and smiling and that these barbarians pay me homage and shout: "Yes, decidedly, Mark Anthony was right, Cleopatra was beautiful."

OLYMPUS
I must admit that the faster death is, the sadder it is, and that the features often remain grimacing and contracted.

CLEOPATRA
And you have no other poison?

OLYMPUS
I know one which provokes progressive numbness of the entire body, then an invincible drowsiness. No spasm, no convulsions, the cheek remains fresh and the soul flees in a smile.

CLEOPATRA
That's exactly what I want!

OLYMPUS
Unfortunately, this sweet end is given by a living creature.

CLEOPATRA
What creature?

OLYMPUS
A serpent; the aspic.

CLEOPATRA
A serpent! What horror! And this poison, cannot you extract it?

OLYMPUS
No.

CLEOPATRA
So, then it's necessary to take the cold beast and feel its sharp teeth? Oh! No, never. Rather this ring since you can find nothing better.

OLYMPUS
Nothing!

(Olympus goes back.)

CLEOPATRA (putting the ring on her finger)
Here I am, affianced to death. It is to this pearl I will have recourse the day you stop loving me.

ANTHONY
I? How mad you are!

CLEOPATRA
Oh! Don't laugh! Black presentiments fly about my face like a swarm of funereal birds. Even last night I had a disturbing dream. I went down the Nile in a boat. I was seated at your feet and wore a diadem. Suddenly this miserable Thryseus, whom you refuse to distrust—

ANTHONY
Truly, no.

CLEOPATRA
Appeared on the river and made a signal to an eagle flying in the heavens. The eagle landed on me, forcefully trying to tear the diadem from me and my sadness was so great that it woke me up.

ANTHONY
Are you going to let yourself be disturbed by a dream? Come on, chase away these black thoughts, my love! And, while waiting for the sun to go down and for Cleopatra to become Diana the Huntress, let's taste the pleasure of living while thinking of nothing. Death is at your finger. The day when you pour it in your cup, I will drink it first.

Until then, let's enjoy the gifts made us by the gods. Come, sit near me! Remember these pretty girls, that your melancholy discouraged. And, because it is a question of an eagle, order the amiable Ahoun to play for us the pretty history of Nitocris, the Egyptian with the pretty feet, whose sandals an eagle brought to Pharaoh Ramses and who, being found after much searching became Queen of Egypt under the name of Rhodopis.

CLEOPATRA
It's a nice story, but Ahoun plays it poorly. It's no use for me to tell her.

ANTHONY
Clearly, she will never play the bath scene the way you do.

CHARMIAN (who approaches)
Especially since you never play it before her.

CLEOPATRA
You will see that Charmian is going to beg me to do it.

ANTHONY
She won't be the only one.

IRIS
Mistress!

(All the women join in a supplicating gesture.)

ANTHONY
You see!

CLEOPATRA
You wish it?

ANTHONY
Imperatively!

CLEOPATRA (softly)
What madness.

ANTHONY
Do it for my pleasure.

CHARMIAN
And to this service to the poor Ahoun.

CLEOPATRA (smiling)
Then, so be it! Watch me closely, little one.

(Anthony is seated. Iris and Charmian remain standing near Cleopatra. Kephren looks on from afar. Thryseus is leaning against a column which commands the Sphinx stairway. Cleopatra takes the scarf from Ahoun and, on a sound of curved harps, advances by slow steps, miming the verses as she recites them.)

CLEOPATRA
Everything still sleeps alone.
Nitocris descends with light steps
To the rocks beaten by the river.
Hush! What noise is that?
Was it a bird lost on its way?
Hidden in the rose bushes?
Nitocris listens.
Her veil—stolen, her tunic slips and falls to her feet.
Hands on her throat, Nitocris shivers,

Throws off her sandals
And slowly plunges into the Nile
And swims Naked on the waves.
The current carries her
And she is beautiful
In the eyes of a delighted King.
But the eagle above,
What's he doing? My sandal.
And taking her fortune for her disgrace,
She watches the eagle glide into space.

(A noise at the right. A servant enters.)

SERVANT
Master.

ANTHONY
What's this mean? Who's bothering us?

SERVANT
Two of your friends who insist—

ANTHONY (standing)
Two friends! Excuse me, Queen.

(Demetrius and Dercetas enter.)

ANTHONY (seeing them, joyfully)
Demetrius! Dercetas! (running to them) Ah! Dear friends, be welcome and salute the Queen who pardons you for interrupting us at the moment she was entrancing us.

DEMETRIUS (saluting with Dercetas)
May she accept our excuses.

ANTHONY
By Pollux! It is heaven which brings you! Only you were lacking to make my joy complete—but, first of all (to slaves), some seats! And some wine! I don't always know, friends, how to offer it to you soaked in snow, but we have other ways of refreshing you. (to Demetrius who looks at the columns of the palace) Demetrius is asking where we are? Here, dear friend, is the ancient palace of the old kings of Egypt, whose pillars tell the tale, it appears, of the exploits of a certain Ramses who was the Caesar or Anthony of his time. The Queen reads this fluently, but for me it's a conjuring book. (the wine and the cups are brought) Very good! Here's the wine! Take seats! Very soon, to welcome you, we are going to hunt lions. Then, after the bathing, we will dine on the terrace. The Queen has admirable cooks. You will taste the dishes of the country. They have a way of dealing with sheep, stuffing it with figs, with raisins and pistachio. On my oath, it is excellent! Come, let's drink. How pleased I am to see you.

DEMETRIUS
In this talk I recognize Mark Anthony! But, at first sight, I would have taken you for this Ramses of whom you were speaking.

ANTHONY (laughing)
Oh! Yes, this outfit! You have to accept the ways of the country you live in. It was the opinion of Alexander, and I don't know anything better to do than to imitate him. But, you are not drinking? By Bacchus, drink then. This rising of the Nile must have changed you! Now then—and tomorrow? Tomorrow what will we do? Our intention, dear friends, is to go back up the river to the cataracts, where my slaves have found turquoise mines. You will be with us, that goes without saying, and the whole length of the way, gently rocked, you will breathe forgetfulness in the lotus chalice, so that nothing more will trouble your ears than the delights of this enchanted country.

DEMETRIUS
We are not here to forget, but to make you remember.

ANTHONY
Remember what, just gods?

DERCETAS
Don't jest!

DEMETRIUS
And listen to grave news.

ANTHONY
Oh, thanks a lot! Not today, not ever! If your news is grave, keep it to yourselves.

DEMETRIUS
Whether you wish it or not, you will hear it.

ANTHONY (starting)
Huh?

DEMETRIUS
Leave these buffoons and Cleopatra! What I have to tell you won't please her.

ANTHONY
By Hercules, you dare?

CLEOPATRA
What are you doing? Since when does one take the messenger for the message? Put Demetrius at his ease. Separate all the others.

ANTHONY
But—

CLEOPATRA
Let them leave us!

(Iris, Charmian, Kephren, the Egyptian Officers, clowns and dancers exit.)

CLEOPATRA
I will remain and I invite Demetrius to speak in all frankness as if he were doing so far from me.

ANTHONY
That's what I will not permit.

CLEOPATRA
I beg you.

ANTHONY
Anyway, I don't want to hear it.

CLEOPATRA
Hear it, and let's find out what this grave news is. Undoubtedly, Octavian is sending you his orders: "Do this or do that."

DEMETRIUS
We do not come on behalf of Octavian.

CLEOPATRA
Then, it's on behalf of Fulvia?

DEMETRIUS
Queen!

CLEOPATRA
Perhaps, you must not stay here very long. Fulvia won't permit it.

ANTHONY
And, what does this woman matter and her complaints?

DEMETRIUS
No outrages today, Anthony!

ANTHONY
What? Am I the only one of my opinion? Fulvia, is she—?

DEMETRIUS
Fulvia is dead.

ANTHONY
Fulvia?

DEMETRIUS
She is dead.

DERCETAS
And, died calling for you.

(A second of silence.)

ANTHONY (falling into his chair)
A great soul has departed.

DEMETRIUS
The gods be praised! Your heart remained faithful to her.

ANTHONY
How does this come about? How is it that, having so many times cursed and almost wished this could happen, I cannot learn of this news coldly? Without bitterness and without regrets?

DEMETRIUS
It's that you remember her violence came from suffering, and that she died in her empty home, faithful to her love for you. Until her last hour, she expected you, a friend having made her hope of your return. Then, feeling death approach, and that the joy of seeing you would be prevented, she murmured: "It's finished. He will never return. It's over for me. It's over for Rome." And her imperious eyes filled with tears. One time more, she repeated your name "Mark

Anthony" in a sweet childish voice which we hardly recognized. This was her last breath.

ANTHONY (after a silence)
So, she said "It's over for Rome"?

DERCETAS
Twice.

ANTHONY
Why these words? Was she babbling in a fever? Or, must one believe, as they assure us, that the future is unveiled to the dying?

DEMETRIUS
Don't doubt it! Rome is lost!

ANTHONY
Rome.

DEMETRIUS
Unless you save it!

ANTHONY (under the watchful eyes of Cleopatra and Thryseus)
I? From what peril?

DEMETRIUS
Are you ignorant of it? This lotus flower—have you breathed it so much that the rest of the world no longer exists for you? Learn then that Sextus Pompey, whose audacity only you can master, again oppresses the sea from the Euxine to the Pillars of Hercules. But, this time, it is not enough for him to sow terror on the coasts of Italy, for his hate against Rome, he is attacking the ships which bring us wheat from Sicily and Africa!

ANTHONY
It will be famine in less than a month!

DERCETAS
He's boasting of it.

ANTHONY (standing)
Then, you are right. Rome has never been in greater peril.

DEMETRIUS
Since the Gauls, no.

ANTHONY (agitated)
And, to save it, you count on me?

DERCETAS
Are we wrong?

ANTHONY (after a moment's hesitation)
Well, well, yes, you are wrong. Yes!

DERCETAS
Is it possible?

DEMETRIUS
You!

ANTHONY
When we, Octavian and I, divided the world, he took Rome and Italy. It's up to him to defend his share. The day Asia is threatened, I will not ask for his help. Let him spare my help. I will spare his.

THRYSEUS
That's the way to speak!

ANTHONY
Too long I needed him at Philippi and against the Parthians, giving me all the trouble and leaving him all the profits. I've indeed conquered the right to rest in peace and if I tarry in Memphis like Han-

nibal in Capua, I defy this teetotaler himself to make a crime of it now that Fulvia is dead.

THRYSEUS
That's so.

DEMETRIUS
So, you are indifferent to the miseries of Rome, and by your inaction, you will serve the cause of its worst enemy?

DERCETAS
You will, let it be said, that not only are you the ally of Cleopatra, but of Sextus Pompey.

DEMETRIUS
That, for the love of a barbarian (movement by Anthony that Cleopatra calms with a gesture), you do what Coriolanus did from scorn, Hannibal from hate?

ANTHONY
And, who will say that? Octavian, right? Yes, by the gods! That's it exactly! I see him. I hear him, filling the Forum with his indignant exclamations, running from one to another with tears in his voice: "Well, do you know the news? Anthony is more than ever dominated by this Queen. The gold of our provinces, the blood of our soldiers, the glory of our arms, he places it all at her feet! Such a great Captain!" And the imbeciles will soften: "Poor Octavian! How he loves him. He weeps over him" Actor!

THRYSEUS
Ah! That's, indeed, the word!

ANTHONY
Well, know it, finally! He exasperates me, in the end, this young trickster draped in his wise hypocrisy, this imperturbable pedant, that nature created to be a schoolmaster and whose fortune is to be the heir of a hero. He disgusts me, this adolescent who has neither

the virtues nor the vices of youth, who, at the age one gets drunk, is sober, where one loves, feels nothing, where one squanders, he hoards. I scorn him no more than he disdains me. I hate him as much as he curses me. But I, at least, I have the audacity of my scorn and the frankness of my hate.

DEMETRIUS
And this hate will go so far as to deprive Rome of your help?

ANTHONY
Rome deserves it. Rome unleashed him and joined the chorus with him against me—against the Queen! Well, by the gods! Here's a great opportunity for him to justify the love of the Romans for him and to witness the heirs of the great Caesar! Let's see the work of this valiant hero and how he profited from the lessons of Thryseus on the school bench.

THRYSEUS (laughing)
Oh! Oh! Very pretty!

ANTHONY
Octavian and Sextus are at war! But, it's a true festival for me to contemplate this joust and, score the blows, by Pollux, I am curious to see who will win—the magistrate or the pirate! And I would, indeed, laugh, if the son of Pompey took vengeance on the nephew of Caesar for Pharsalus.

CLEOPATRA (tranquilly, without budging)
No! You wouldn't laugh. (all, surprised, turn attentively to her) For, after all, it's with Sextus Pompey that you have a score. Don't you think this revenge would fall back on you? Or that he will pardon you for confiscating his father's house? (rising) And, if Octavian wins?

ANTHONY
Impossible!

CLEOPATRA
That was the word that killed Caesar. And, if Octavian wins—will he leave you in peaceable possession of Asia? Has he forgotten his schoolboy anger against Cleopatra? How blind you are. (coming forward) But, he has only one constant thought, this man, but one hope, one vision, which obsesses him. His triumph the day when he brings Rome the strangled cadaver of Anthony, or Cleopatra, barefoot, hands chained, marching behind his chariot, under the cheers of the Roman populace.

ANTHONY
And, you advise me to save such a man?

CLEOPATRA
It's not he that you save. It is Rome. And Rome will recognize you and acclaim you like a god. The blow that strikes Sextus Pompey, strikes Octavian. Your popularity will crush his. And these men, your friends, are not going to shout because the Egyptian Queen puts your valor to sleep that the grandson of Hercules threading a distaff at the feet of another Omphale. They are going to know that Cleopatra puts your glory before her love and that she admires and loves you as the first of all, for being first also, with you. To these Romans, starving today, tomorrow swollen with your victory, they can say: "The wheat arrives for you. It's Cleopatra who sends it to you." And this will be my pride to give bread to these Roman plebeians who will thank me with their ingratitude—but which will make you master of the world.

DEMETRIUS
Glory to you, Queen! I am learning to know you. It was wisdom herself who just spoke.

DERCETAS
Let it please the gods that Anthony have no other advisers than you.

ANTHONY
Yes, she's right. You are right, Queen! It's as well, too. All goes to your honor.

CLEOPATRA
And yours!

ANTHONY
Well, so be it! That's agreed. I will leave, friend. We will leave together. You will lead this hunt with me instead of the other.

DEMETRIUS
Ah, surely.

DERCETAS
And with great heart!

ANTHONY
And you, too Thryseus?

THRYSEUS
Always!

ANTHONY
Give us this last day of pleasure and then, tomorrow—

CLEOPATRA
Tomorrow! It's not tomorrow that you must leave. It's today.

ANTHONY
You wish it?

CLEOPATRA
The hours steal away! They mustn't fight without you and lose everything.

DEMETRIUS (to Dercetas)
Assuredly!

CLEOPATRA
Go instantly! The boat which brought them will take you to Alexandria. Arm the swiftest of my ships and fight Sextus. Triumph over him as over his father and prove to your enemies that you are still Mark Anthony and that you are not less valiant for being loved by a barbarian!

DEMETRIUS
O, Queen!

DERCETAS
Pardon us!

ANTHONY
Let's go! All is said! We are leaving! Eros, my sword, my cuirass! Let my Legionnaires recognize Mark Anthony under the armor!

CLEOPATRA (to Kephren)
And make the boats ready. (to Anthony) By tomorrow, I will equip my fleet and that of my tributaries. At your first call, it will meet you where you tell me.

ANTHONY
In Sicily, without doubt! Anyway, I won't spare you messages.

(Juba and Eros bring the sword and the cuirass.)

CLEOPATRA (to Eros)
Let it alone, child. Today, I replace you and will buckle the cuirass.

ANTHONY (who has already put the cuirass on his back)
With those little hands? You want to?

CLEOPATRA
It will please me; let me do it! What serves this buckle? Ah! I know! And, this other? Is it attached the same way?

ANTHONY
No, the reverse.

CLEOPATRA
It resists!

ANTHONY
Take care not to hurt yourself.

CLEOPATRA
It's done.

ANTHONY
Dear friend!

CLEOPATRA (wiping her fingers)
It's nothing.

ANTHONY
Some blood.

(Anthony takes Cleopatra's hand and presses it to his lips.)

CLEOPATRA (sadly)
If it is a warning! If I never see you again?

ANTHONY
What folly! Between death and me, there is a cuirass buckled by your adored hands.

CLEOPATRA
Ah! How I wish I could imprison your heart in it, and that it was also between you and other women!

ANTHONY
And you have nothing more to fear.

CLEOPATRA
Present, I fear no one—but absent, who knows! It is the Queen who spoke just now, the woman at present! If you were going to betray me for another—

ANTHONY
I? Great gods! And, what other do you want?

CLEOPATRA
You will return to Rome triumphant. All those you once loved, others, too, will offer themselves to you, happy to dispute you with the Egyptian. It was much already that they stole from me your looks. Don't forget the one who sacrificed her joy to your glory and who, in her sad solitude, counts the hours which separate us. Think of those who wait for you, who adore you—and who weep.

ANTHONY
I swear to the gods.

CLEOPATRA
Oh, don't swear! Fulvia's oaths meant nothing! I much prefer a good and simple promise from your heart.

ANTHONY
Fear nothing, my beloved! I intend these Romans who misunderstand you be surprised to see me, so different from myself, and to say: "What woman is this Cleopatra? By what charms is she so adorned and what merits, that he is faithful to her to such a degree." Thus my fidelity will sing your praises, force their esteem and rejoice myself in the homage that I am going to render you before the eyes of Rome entire—through the constancy of my love.

CLEOPATRA
Yes, that's the word I was waiting for. Let me thank the mouth that said it.

(Cleopatra draws herself against Anthony's heart.)

KEPHREN (returning)
Queen, the ships are ready!

CLEOPATRA
Let's go. It's necessary. We will separate. May the stars light your way and victory greet your passage, still and always amorous of you. Goodbye! Goodbye!

ANTHONY
And, why won't you accompany me to Alexandria at least?

CLEOPATRA (wiping away his tears)
Oh, no! That would be another tearing apart down there. I am brave for the moment—you see! Let's profit by it. Leave quickly! Go, then, go!

(Cleopatra makes a sign for him to leave and stays in one place, not looking at him. Anthony, dragged away by Demetrius and Dercetas, escapes and returns to Cleopatra. He takes her in his arms and silently they exchange a long kiss. Then he tears himself from this embrace and leaves quickly. The women go to Cleopatra who is alone.)

CLEOPATRA
Now, send the clowns away! Send away the musicians and the dancers. I no longer want songs, nor laughter, nor flowers, nor perfumes—but rather, silence and mourning until his return I am a widow.

(The servants disperse slowly, silently. Cleopatra goes toward the Sphinx, where, leaning on it, she casts a last glance at Anthony, and with her hand waves him a last goodbye. Then, resting on her elbows, falls in tears.)

CURTAIN

ACT III

Scene 3

A Terrace in Memphis

Night. At the foot of the terrace the sleeping city, bristling with obelisks and pylons ornamented with pennants. The Nile, shining under the moon, snakes between the temples surrounded by palms, then spreads in the plain, lost to view, where the Sphinx and pyramids rise up.

A large awning sustained by pillars of bronze screens the bed set in the corner of the terrace on which Cleopatra is stretched as if drowsy. Iris and Charmian, seated on the steps, watch her. Kephren, in an almost royal outfit, watches with two archers, at the door which dominates the terrace. The Diviner, seated on the near wall, considers the stars, and all low, dictates the cipher to a scribe dressed in a black skirt drawn in with white corselets. A festive music rises from the Nile, in the midst of the Nile's silence. The two women rise and listen, leaning on the balustrade of the terrace, their gaze turned toward the Nile.

CHARMIAN
Clement Isis! Since the Queen does not wake—Kephren. (to a slave) Go down to the river quickly! And, on the part of Kephren, order these people to shut up.

(The slave bows.)

CLEOPATRA (raising her hand)
No, wait!

A VOICE
The evening wind carries the palm seeds. The evening wind carries perfume. O, my Isis, Raise your veils, Reveal husband to wife And wife to husband. O, my Isis. Come! Only the stars see your master at your knees.

CLEOPATRA
What are those ships?

CHARMIAN
Gracious Queen, it's the cortege of the Scribe Khafri. The priests of Hathor have celebrated the engagement this morning—and he is bringing his new wife home.

CLEOPATRA
And who is Khafri's spouse?

IRIS
It's the pretty Neferti, the daughter of the Head Librarian.

CLEOPATRA (sighing)
Happy Neferti. She marries one who she loves and nothing but death will separate her from him. Kephren! Order the protector of the treasure to choose the shiniest of my enamel necklaces. Tomorrow morning, you will bring it from me yourself to Neferti. Tell her I send it to her and wish her never to know the torments of absence. Beg her to ask the gods for the return of Mark Anthony.

(Kephren bows without replying.)

IRIS (to herself)
Poor Kephren! Won't he ever be free, he especially, loving someone who does not love him.

(Kephren, after a word to a slave who goes off, takes his place by the door. The music fades. Cleopatra rises in the attitude of a sphinx and searches the horizon.)

CLEOPATRA
Always nothing! How far can my eyes see? Nothing but couples tarrying, walking slowly and, at each kiss, taking the stars as witness for their love. And the Diviner? What's he doing?

CHARMIAN
He's finishing his mystic calculation.

CLEOPATRA (hanging her head)
Ah, if at least while waiting for him to finish, I could sleep for an hour!

IRIS
Try again, Queen of Beauty!

CLEOPATRA
Queen of Sadness.

CHARMIAN
Close your sweet eyes! We will watch in your place, and, if a messenger appears, we will inform you of it.

CLEOPATRA
He will never come again. It's finished.

(Cleopatra stretches out on the cushions, eyes closed.)

DIVINER (low to Scribe)
Repeat with me the sacred formula. (rising, their arms toward heaven they begin to pray) Osiris, King of Day. Osiris, King of the world! Osiris, soul of heaven, all the shadows of Typhon cannot dim your splendor.

OLYMPUS (outside)
Make way!

KEPHREN (quickly without voice)
Who goes there? (Olympus appears; he throws himself on him) Don't move, if you value your life.

OLYMPUS
What? Are you going to harm me? Don't you recognize me?

KEPHREN
Olympus!

IRIS
Finally.

KEPHREN (low)
Excuse me, old man. I thought you were shut in the crypt of the temple and your appearances are so rare! I wasn't expecting you!

OLYMPUS
Right! But, is that a reason to take me by the throat?

(Charmian comes to him.)

CHARMIAN
Be happy that he let you go so quickly. The last messenger from Anthony, Kephren almost strangled.

OLYMPUS
How's that?

CHARMIAN
Oh, I don't know—something about Octavian. Kephren's got it in his head that Octavian intends to kill the Queen.

OLYMPUS
Octavian has no interest in the Queen dying.

CHARMIAN
On the contrary. However, it may be Kephren, since he was promoted to governor of this palace, has reclaimed the honor of watching over Cleopatra, as when he was the first of her guards. All night he marches them past her doors. One night, near the same hour as now, a messenger arrived, preceded by one of the slaves and both rushed up the stairs. Kephren thought it was an affair of assassins. He seized the slave by the throat. If he hadn't recognized his error in time the man was dead! This happened two months ago. That was the last news the Queen has received from the Triumvir. And for two months our mistress has languished, each day more pale. It's what I prayed they inform you about.

OLYMPUS
You've done well.

CHARMIAN (bringing him near the bed)
Look at her!

OLYMPUS (low)
Is she sleeping?

CLEOPATRA
Who is speaking? It's you, worthy Olympus! Those who have taken you from your patient studies have bothered you in vain. No, I am not sleeping. My eyes don't wish to sleep, nor cry; my mouth is on fire as if I had eaten fruits of the Sycamore; my heart beats in my breast like a captive bird's, but neither the sugar of the mandrake, nor amulets calm my fever or appease my heart. What will cure me is a messenger from Anthony, running here on the highway, or even an ibis, coming to land on the terrace with a papyrus attached to his wing. But, you see, nothing appears. Neither on the road nor in the heavens! During the first days of his absence, one of his couriers or one of my birds brought me daily a tender letter. Then, the letters

became rarer. Then he dictated them instead of writing them himself. Then, no more news of him came. No more than if not one of my darling ibises had escaped from vultures. The messengers that I have sent from hour to hour, have they been unable to reach him? Has he left the land of Africa? Have his messengers been stopped by the pirates or held up by storms? The month that we are entering is one during which the rages of Typhon are the most dreadful to sailors.

OLYMPUS
It is true. And that alone suffices to explain—

CLEOPATRA (exalting)
Or bold, as always, has Anthony been wounded in combat? Is he dead of his wounds? And, is he trying to hide it from me?

CHARMIAN
Can you think—?

CLEOPATRA
Oh, yes, I know him! The remedy will be quickly found. I won't have any trouble throwing this pearl in my cup.

OLYMPUS
Queen! In the name of Egypt!

CLEOPATRA
And say that that's it! And that he's dead. I, I'm the one who killed him.

OLYMPUS
You?

CLEOPATRA
Didn't I make him leave, in spite of himself? And why? Great gods! For the applause of the Romans! Stupid pride! Inconceivable folly!

CHARMIAN
Be silent, I beg you.

CLEOPATRA
He would still be here! Me at his feet, as you are at mine. And between two kisses, he would tell me: "Suppose we went to sing the Epithalamium at the door of newlyweds." And we will go, holding hands, suddenly changing our idea on the way, and run to some new mad adventure! Ah, those times, those times when I joked with him, just to make him lose patience, when I would wake so I could see him in his turn and his sword at his side when he called me his Serpent of the Nile.

OLYMPUS
Those times will come again, sweet Queen.

CLEOPATRA
How's that?

OLYMPUS
When Anthony returns.

CLEOPATRA
Fine. But—

OLYMPUS
Anthony loves you. You don't doubt it?

CLEOPATRA
May the gods preserve me from it.

OLYMPUS
Who knows that he has not already triumphed over Sextus? Who knows if he isn't reserving the pleasure of being the first to tell you? Who knows if he isn't on the way back already?

CLEOPATRA (ardently)
Ah, yes, return! Return quickly! In Memphis, once so joyous, all call you, all await you, from the granite gods who dream with hands on their knees, to the crouching sphinxes down there on the horizon. Return, if you have understood how I love you. Hasten, if you pity me. I am dying of calling you, night and day, and of calling you in vain.

OLYMPUS
Queen! Contain yourself.

CLEOPATRA (wildly)
And, how can I? Everything exasperates my mourning, the visions that haunt me, the breezes that pass, coming from the desert, the echo of other's joy, determined to pursue me.

(The music rises again. Kephren goes to renew his order to a slave. She stops.)

CLEOPATRA
I forbid you to budge! It pleases me to see how they mock me.

IRIS
Mistress!

CLEOPATRA (bitterly)
Ah! I wish everything in Egypt was as sad as I am, for the pleasure of refusing them all my complaints. (to Kephren) I forbid you.

KEPHREN (with a sigh)
So be it!

CLEOPATRA
Nothing changes sadness! I know your thoughts.

KEPHREN
What?

CLEOPATRA
And the joy that hides your silence and the fear you have of seeing Anthony return.

KEPHREN
I?

CLEOPATRA (getting worked up)
If suffices. A man that I have overwhelmed with honors, to whom I have given my scepter to carry! How could I have blinded myself to such a degree?

IRIS (timidly)
Sweet Queen.

CLEOPATRA
You are going to speak to me on his behalf? When I tell you they all betray me! Let's begin with this astrologer.

DIVINER
Poor goddesses.

CLEOPATRA
Have you done anything? And since you began to twist your neck to decipher the hieroglyphics of the night—what response have you been able to read and are you going to give me?

DIVINER
If you think me capable—

CLEOPATRA
Of nothing! You are only a blind fool, an ass that one saddles and unsaddles.

DIVINER (gravely)
Take care! In insulting me, you insult the gods! Moreover, I have proven my science with a hundred prodigies. And I do my best to

protect you against the dangers of water and the stings of arrows, and to teach you the spell which charms heaven and earth and discloses the perils of the future with regard to the living.

CLEOPATRA
I don't care about all that! Tell me only, where is Mark Anthony?

DIVINER
Mark Anthony must have left Africa.

CLEOPATRA
Evidently, since we no longer see the ibis and the ibis doesn't fly across the sea. There is no need to be an astrologer to know that. But, if he has left Africa, where is he now? In Sicily? In Italy?

DIVINER
I cannot tell.

CLEOPATRA
So well have you divined the future, that you are ignorant of the present?

DIVINER
I have followed Horus, the speaking guide of space across the region of the wandering stars and the fixed stars. Horus has shown me the purple-red star of the god of war retrograding toward a lesser star whose glitter is cold like a diamond.

CLEOPATRA (attentively)
Do I understand you? You mean Anthony's fortune pales before that of Octavian?

DIVINER
I have often advised Anthony not to fight this young man. And Anthony himself admitted he has never played dice with him without losing.

CLEOPATRA
In short, the responses of heaven are disturbing?

DIVINER
They have been for some time, but I have so often renewed the gift offerings that the gods have finally been appeased. The shadow lightens, the symbols are clarifying. In rereading my calculations I have found signs of peace.

CLEOPATRA
That's fine!

DIVINER
I see Anthony mixing at a festival.

CLEOPATRA
A triumph?

DIVINER
Perhaps. And yet, this festival is not a celebration of war. Rather one would say it is a religious ceremony.

CLEOPATRA
Of what type?

DIVINER (following the scribe's notes)
The figures don't say. But we are going to know. News is on its way.

CLEOPATRA
Is this true?

DIVINER
According to the ways of earth and heaven!

CLEOPATRA
And, the news is good?

DIVINER
It will be if it comes before the sixth hour of the night. After the sixth hour, the omens are funereal.

CLEOPATRA
And, the sixth hour approaches. Look, the shadow of the pyramids turns already.

KEPHREN (leaning on the terrace, quickly)
Mistress! Look down there. At the corner of the temple, that man running with his cloak on his arms.

CLEOPATRA (shouting)
A messenger. It's one of mine.

CHARMIAN
Finally!

DIVINER
What did I say?

CLEOPATRA (who leans on the wall)
Quickly! Quickly! Over here! Show him the route, you others. You see, they were letting him turn by the terrace. No! He knows his way. Kephren! My faithful Kephren, watch so no one dares delay him. (Kephren disappears) And you, worthy Diviner, precious head, pardon me my rage and name your reward. (the Diviner bows) Ah, good Olympus! There's the remedy I needed.

(Kephren reappears leading the messenger, an Egyptian, hair braided, tunic held by a camel hair cord. Two slaves accompany him.)

CLEOPATRA
Quickly! Good servant! Here! Come here!

MESSENGER
Queen!

(The Messenger prostrates himself, elbows at his knees, hands on the flagstones, breathless, trembling.)

CLEOPATRA (shocked)
What am I going to learn? Ah, Charmian, how frightened I am.

MESSENGER
Queen, who holds the scepter and the whip. Queen, who holds nations beneath your ivory talons.

CLEOPATRA
It suffices! Anthony is dead. Take care! To say that is to kill me. You don't wish that, right? Tell me that he is living and that he loves me more than ever. Tell me that, and these bracelets are yours and I allow you to kiss the blue veins of this hand where Kings have placed their trembling lips.

MESSENGER
Anthony lives and has no thought of dying.

CLEOPATRA (removing her bracelets)
Here! This for your trouble. And this, too. But, then give up this somber face which announces nothing good. Speak, without my having to tear the words from you. You have seen Anthony.

MESSENGER
I have seen him.

CLEOPATRA
Where?

MESSENGER
In Rome.

CLEOPATRA
So, it's from Rome you come? And what's he doing in Rome?

MESSENGER
I thought to come through Alexandria. A tempest the most formidable that Typhon has unleashed tossed our ship on the coast of Cyrenaica and that is why I arrive so late.

CLEOPATRA
What do you reproach yourself for? I ask you why Mark Anthony is at Rome. Is Rome still threatened by Sextus?

MESSENGER
No, truly! Rome is delivered from that menace forever.

CLEOPATRA
Speak then.

MESSENGER
The enemies of Anthony maintained that the honor belongs only to Agrippa, the Lieutenant of Octavian, and that Mark Anthony came to Sicily after the battle was already won. The truth is, the last battles were decisive, and it was Mark Anthony who forced Sextus to surrender and all his fleet with him.

CLEOPATRA
Ah, valiant Anthony! I see now that you are devoted to me! You will make your fortune with me.

MESSENGER
At the end of this victory, Anthony, Octavian, and Sextus met in Sicily where they signed a treaty of alliance.

CLEOPATRA
Anthony? With Octavian?

MESSENGER
Yes, the division of the conquered fleet even caused quarrels, Anthony declaring he wanted to keep the largest part.

CLEOPATRA
Why not keep it all?

MESSENGER
In short, the friends of Anthony intervened and the friends of Octavian—and finally, Octavian's sister herself—the sweet Octavia.

CLEOPATRA
Well?

MESSENGER
And, thanks to her good offices, an accord has been signed between them.

CLEOPATRA
I do not like that.

MESSENGER
Must I continue?

CLEOPATRA
What more have you to tell me?

MESSENGER
Gracious Queen! But, first of all, know that I have only seen Anthony from a distance. He has not spoken to me. But, what remains to be told comes not from him, but rather from his secretary.

CLEOPATRA
Thryseus?

MESSENGER
Yes.

CLEOPATRA
Then, it is death you bring me?

MESSENGER
Think!

CLEOPATRA
Well! Go! Finish me with a single blow. Anthony has promised not to return to Egypt?

MESSENGER
No, sweet Queen, no. The promise he made is to another.

CLEOPATRA
I don't understand.

MESSENGER
To seal the peace which was engineered by the intervention of the noble sister of Octavian—

CLEOPATRA
He loves her?

MESSENGER
I cannot say if he loves her.

CLEOPATRA
Octavia!

MESSENGER
I only know he married her.

CLEOPATRA
Her! Get out, wretch! Out of here! Away from me!

MESSENGER (seized by fear and falling nearly prostrate)
Mistress!

CLEOPATRA (putting her foot on the shoulder of the crouching Messenger)
Stay there—and admit you have lied. If not, this gold I have given you, I will melt it and put it, boiling, down your throat!

MESSENGER
I have told the truth.

CLEOPATRA
So, you persist?

MESSENGER
Alas, I wasn't the one who performed the marriage.

CLEOPATRA
Again! Ah! Dog! Let him be killed.

CHARMIAN
Queen! An innocent!

CLEOPATRA
Him! Rods! Whip him with rods of iron. Then, throw him in a pit full of serpents. No. He would die too quickly. Keep him there, under heavy guard. I will invent a punishment for him. (Kephren makes the messenger leave.) Married! He is married! He, who swore by my eyes, by my lips, never to know other kisses than mine. Married! What a surprise he kept for me. This feast you saw him occupied with, too clairvoyant diviner, it was a wedding feast. Execrable treason.

CHARMIAN
Who knows how—?

CLEOPATRA
Oh, I ought to have foreseen it! From the few tears he shed over Fulvia, I ought to have understood how it would be with me. Married! To that woman! While I languish in solitude, in the broken

memory of joys past, asking myself: "Where is he?" and imagining him full of me, he was getting married. Before Rome all assembled, he brought her to his home, and then rehearsed to her the words he wasted on me, and weeping of love in her arms. Ah, coward! Coward! Coward!

CHARMIAN
Queen, hear me!

CLEOPATRA
The sister of Octavian! Is it believable? Has he taken a wife from the hands of his worst enemy?

CHARMIAN
Clearly he didn't do it from love. What he did, he must have had secret reasons for doing it. Who knows what this secret reconciliation hides? And if this marriage is not a trick?

CLEOPATRA
And their kisses—are they a trick, too? What senseless hope makes you seem to think that? Why do you say he does not love her? Perhaps, Octavia is very loveable. She is, in the words of this messenger, who couldn't help calling her "the sweet Octavia".

CHARMIAN
Are you going to believe that on a word?

CLEOPATRA
Still, I want to be sure of it. You are right. A word is not enough. Kephren, loyal Kephren, bring that man back.

KEPHREN
You wish?

CLEOPATRA
Let him come! He has nothing more to fear from me.

(Kephren goes to find the Messenger, who is held by two slaves.)

KEPHREN
Approach!

(The Messenger comes forward.)

CLEOPATRA
And speak boldly. I am no longer angry with you. It was not you who lied.

MESSENGER
From misfortune.

CLEOPATRA
Come here. And do not lie! For, if I catch you in a lie, you are dead. Tell me, this Octavia that Anthony has married—you've seen her?

MESSENGER
Yes, redoubtable Queen.

CLEOPATRA
Very close?

MESSENGER
As close as I see you.

CLEOPATRA
Where was that?

MESSENGER
In the Forum, when she was walking between her brother and her husband.

CLEOPATRA
Gods! Ah, gods! What's she like? Tall.

MESSENGER
Enough!

CLEOPATRA
Ah!

MESSENGER
Less than you, Queen, much less.

CLEOPATRA
Good! And, you heard her speak? Has she a sharp voice or a grave one?

MESSENGER
Rather heavy.

CLEOPATRA (to Charmian)
For a woman, that's not so graceful.

CHARMIAN (leaning)
Yes, ridiculous figure, heavy voice.

CLEOPATRA
All this wouldn't be very remarkable. (to Messenger) And her gait?

MESSENGER
Her gait is slow.

IRIS
She drags herself.

MESSENGER
Like this.

CLEOPATRA
So, not majestic.

MESSENGER
Far from it.

CHARMIAN
And, there are not three men in Egypt at most that could judge her.

CLEOPATRA
In fact, she seems intelligent. How old do you think she is?

MESSENGER
Oh! She is no longer very young. And, without the paint with which she covers her cheeks—

CLEOPATRA (to Charmian and Iris, delighted)
She paints! You hear?

MESSENGER
Outrageously!

CLEOPATRA (to messenger)
And her face? You remember her face? Is it oval, elongated or round?

MESSENGER (while watching Cleopatra's face)
Wait, Queen, I remember. Excessively round.

CLEOPATRA
That is certainly not a mark of wit.

IRIS
Evidently.

CHARMIAN
She is a fool.

CLEOPATRA
As all the virtuous! Her eyes shine, right?

MESSENGER
Dead.

CLEOPATRA
And her hair? Doubtless, blonde?

MESSENGER
Of a blonde dye.

(Laughs and exclamations of the women.)

CLEOPATRA (removing a jewel)
Perhaps, she is blonde? Wait! Take this and don't take offense over my upset just now. I intend to give you employment in the palace. (to slaves) Let him be refreshed and take great care of him! Great care!

MESSENGER (bowing)
Generous Mistress.

(The Messenger leaves proudly, followed by several slaves.)

CLEOPATRA (breathing)
Come now! If I believe this man, this creature will be no great thing.

CHARMIAN
Say that she is nothing.

CLEOPATRA
And, surely he has seen truly beautiful women. He must know what he's saying.

CHARMIAN
If he's seen some! Good Isis! He's been in your service a long while.

CLEOPATRA
The question is to know if he didn't lie. He is very capable of it.

IRIS
Can you think so?

CLEOPATRA
No! It's resolved. I will only believe my eyes.

CHARMIAN
How?

CLEOPATRA
I feel that I won't be able to live until I have seen this woman.

CHARMIAN and IRIS
You think?

CLEOPATRA (threatening the horizon)
Ah, you think you are safe because the abyss of the sea separates us? And you laugh at me, with her? If the sea were blown by the breath of Typhon, I would cross it to see this Octavia, that you prefer to Cleopatra! (to Kephren) A ship. Have a ship fitted with selected rowers. And, when I have seen her, I want to leave in less than an hour. Ah! Why don't I have wings? (stopping) Wait a moment. Look, then, Charmian. Isn't that an ibis that brushes the terrace there?

CHARMIAN and IRIS
Yes, Mistress.

CLEOPATRA
Was it this messenger who must come across the heavens? It's him. He's coming right here. What other news has he come to bring me? There, he stops and seems to hesitate? What is it that frightens him? Some vulture? No, it's an eagle which pursues him. Kephren, take this bow— Too late! The eagle is on him and drags him in his claws.

Never mind. At risk of killing the ibis, I must have the message he brings me. (Kephren holds the bow, the arrow whistles aloft) That's it. Very good. It's fallen. Run! (Slaves hurry out) Was it the eagle who killed it? The eagle of my dream, still and always.

(Kephren returns with the ibis, wings covered with red blood.)

CLEOPATRA
Let's see. Give it here. Sweet thing, still shivering. (searches in the feathers) What? Nothing? Yes? Here's a letter. Sealed with his seal. (opening and reading) "The Triumvir, Anthony, to Queen Cleopatra—from Carthage. Arm your war fleet and leave for Actium."

CHARMIAN
Nothing more?

CLEOPATRA
Nothing.

CHARMIAN
What's it mean?

CLEOPATRA
So—he's left Rome? He's going to give battle! Against whom? Against Octavian. They are still enemies—and then Octavia. Ah, that's what we need to know. (to Kephren) Sound the alarm and arm your marines. Send the order to the ships at Alexandria to depart. You, make me pass for dying. So that Egypt will still think I am at Memphis, while I am going down there to clip the claws of the Roman eagle. (starts to leave, then stops) Ah, Charmian, give this ibis to Phraor, Intendant of the Palace Embalmers, and have him not spare this mummy neither perfumes nor rich bandages. I want it to be reborn one day with me—the faithful messenger who gave me its life.

CURTAIN

ACT IV

Scene 4

Actium

A vast Greek house, filled with statues, and dominating the narrow pass which precedes the Gulf of Ambracia. Through a large semi-circular bay window opening on a terrace one can see the sea all blue and the river of Epirus crowned by temples. A flotilla of tall triremes is anchored at the foot of the rocks. The sky is pure, the sun is setting on the horizon. In the middle of the arch, and fully in view on three stones steps sits a wooden pyre formed by axes circled by great crowns painted and garlanded with oaks and laurels. At the foot of the wooden pyre lean the fasces of the lictors. All around stacked fanwise are the eagles and standards of the Romans. In the midst rises a lance and a crown of olives. In the interior of the wooden pyre a trophy which is seen only when the pyre flames. It is made of a strong iron shank, having at its summit a cassock under a coat of armor and a sword suspended from a baldric. Another iron work forms the branches of a cross with, on its extended arms, two bucklers on each side—crossed and in their midst three javelins. To the right, seats before a table. To the left a bed enveloped in floating material. Under the observation of Strepsiades, slaves decorate with flowers, place the seats. Outside legionnaires watch.

STREPSIADES
Still more flowers here! Myrtles preferably, since it's a seat for new-lyweds. And always join myrtles and laurels. (coming to the bed)

Let's see! Are they sufficiently protected against the breezes of the night? It needs more. One more blanket there. This palace that Sulla built before he died has never been occupied. Here you can see everything. The Divine Anthony could have found at Actium a less sumptuous dwelling, but not one where everything could be improvised. What are you doing here? Go, occupy yourself with fresh wine for dinner.

SLAVE
Does Mark Anthony sup with all his friends or only with Octavian?

STREPSIADES
That's what we would like to know. While waiting, go. And don't make friends with Octavian's servants.

SLAVE
Me?

STREPSIADES
Are you going to go? (the slave leaves) You—go find me on the ship in question the Babylonian tapestry which I spoke to you about—and you will put it there. (pointing to the foot of the bed)

(The slaves begin to leave. At this moment Demetrius appears on the terrace overlooking the sea. Dellius, Dercetas and Juba are with him.)

STREPSIADES
You will wait to bring him until I give you the sign.

(Thryseus also enters. Above, coming and going—Geminus, Ventidius and Cassidius. Outside, but in view, other officers.)

DEMETRIUS (to Dellius)
And where did you get this news from?

DELLIUS
From the intendant that's here.

DEMETRIUS (to Strepsiades)
So, you have seen an Egyptian ship land?

STREPSIADES
From this side, through an archers' opening. And the owner of the ship told me he preceded the fleet of Cleopatra.

DELLIUS
You hear him?

DEMETRIUS
And, where is this ship?

STREPSIADES
The same place I saw it. In a little cove of the river—at the foot of the promontory of Actium.

DERCETAS
If we were to question this man?

STREPSIADES
Useless! He is not going to tell you anything more.

JUBA
Is Anthony aware of it?

DELLIUS
Yes. He went to the temple of Apollo with Octavian precisely to see if the fleet of Cleopatra had arrived.

(Strepsiades goes back, eye and ear on the alert.)

DEMETRIUS
Well! I continue to think Cleopatra's fleet won't arrive.

THRYSEUS (excitedly)
Right?

DELLIUS
Still, why did this Egyptian tell us so?

DEMETRIUS
Who knows to what end?

DELLIUS
You think for some treasonable purpose?

DEMETRIUS
From Cleopatra? What have we better to expect? She cannot ignore accomplished facts. She knows that Agrippa, by attacking the fleet of Sextus Pompey before we came, and by profiting from this victory that we wanted for ourselves, has put Anthony in the position of being obliged to reconcile with a triumphant adversary. She knows that Anthony must have given in to the pressure of all the Roman people who, to better seal the accord, demanded his marriage with Octavian's sister. And this marriage, you who know Cleopatra, can you believe she has learned of it without rage?

THRYSEUS (laughing)
Ah, I can see her from here, the Egyptian! A true fury!

DELLIUS
So be it. But, she also knows that peace hasn't lasted long. That the rupture between these enemy brothers is definitive, and that their armies are only waiting for a signal to come to blows.

DERCETAS
Well? What does he matter now, to Cleopatra?

DELLIUS
If the break is definitive between the brother and Octavia's husband—won't Octavia be the first victim of these discords?

DEMETRIUS
Would Anthony send her back to Octavian?

DELLIUS
And, why not? The peace broken, the alliance which is meant to affirm it, has no reason to exist. See that bridge of boats down there, which, from one promontory to the other, links two armies and permits some brave people to go from camp to camp and attempt a supreme effort of conciliation before giving battle. That bridge then is a last link, a very fragile one, between the separated members of the Roman State. Three blows of an axe would be enough to destroy it. To the very chaste and very pious Octavia, but three words from Anthony, "I repudiate you," will send her to the misery of her deserted hearth. Cleopatra is counting on it.

DERCETAS
She's wrong.

(Unanimous approval.)

DELLIUS
Why is that?

DERCETAS
Because Anthony is very sincerely in love with his young wife.

DELLIUS
He says it often.

DERCETAS
Besides, it's enough to see her.

DELLIUS
Right. I hope it is true. He loves her. But, how? And for how long? Ah, dear friends, which of us has not savored as he does the contrast between a timid spouse and a bold courtesan? After a month of orgies, it's delicious to taste fresh water. "Ah, that's the best of drinks.

I don't want anything more." But, when the slave obediently presents it to me for supper, "Some wine, by Bacchus, some wine." And I throw the fresh water in his face!

DEMETRIUS
This story signifies?

DELLIUS
That Octavia is pure water and that Cleopatra is one of those heady wines that makes us say and do stupid things—which one ceaselessly curses, but always returns to. I saw Anthony there, just now, on the rocks with his young wife questioning the horizon and sucking in the wind full of marine odors and I thought, "Does he breathe the evening breeze? Or the intoxicating perfumes come from distant Egypt."

DEMETRIUS
I have a better opinion of him.

(Movement in the distance. The officers call each other. Noise of voices.)

DERCETAS
What is it?

AN OFFICER (in the distance)
The fleet.

ALL
The Egyptian fleet?

OFFICERS (in the distance)
Yes! Yes! The fleet!

(They quickly go up to watch the sea. Great excitement. Noise of officers and soldiers running.)

THRYSEUS (agitated)
Impossible.

DEMETRIUS
Look!

DERCETAS (to a soldier)
Run! Warn Mark Anthony.

(The soldier runs off.)

DELLIUS (going back with them)
Fine! He must have seen it before us.

THRYSEUS (alone, aside)
Cleopatra's fleet! That's bad for us, both Octavian and me. How to sow discord between Mark Anthony and the Queen of Egypt that the fleet will go back to sea? There it is, Thryseus—now you must call on all your genius.

(Thryseus goes to the terrace. Strepsiades, seeing them all occupied at the back, goes to draw the curtains which shut out the bay. Then comes to the door and calls in a low voice.)

STREPSIADES (over the confused noise outside)
Enter! No one will notice you. (some slaves enter carrying a long tapestry, soft and decorated with rolls of silk) Put this tapestry where I told you. (the slaves put it softly on the bed) Now, go.

(The slaves leave. Some trumpets sound in the distance. Cleopatra emerges from the tapestry and gives her hand to Strepsiades)

CLEOPATRA
Your dagger! (he gives her the dagger with which she finishes pulling herself from her cords. Low to Strepsiades) No one suspects anything?

STREPSIADES
No one.

CLEOPATRA
Anthony?

STREPSIADES
He's going to come.

CLEOPATRA
Octavia is here?

STREPSIADES
Yes, Queen.

CLEOPATRA
This is their lodging?

STREPSIADES
Since this morning.

CLEOPATRA (finding on the bed a gold mirror)
Since this morning? Or since last night?

STREPSIADES (hesitating)
Since the siesta hour.

CLEOPATRA
Ah, damn them!

STREPSIADES
Queen.

CLEOPATRA (excitedly)
Listen.

ANTHONY (outside)
Ah, glory to the gods!

CLEOPATRA
It's Anthony!

STREPSIADES (coming to the hangings)
With her.

CLEOPATRA
Now, I am going to see her?

ANTHONY (gaily)
The beautiful naked birds of Egypt.

(The curtains of the bay are raised before him. Anthony appears in the midst of his lieutenants. Octavia is leaning tenderly on his arm. They come down slowly, speaking with the officers who surround them, while Cleopatra hides herself from seeing the face of Octavia behind the curtains of the bed.)

ANTHONY
Well? Demetrius, you who said this fleet wouldn't come?

DEMETRIUS
I don't believe my eyes.

ANTHONY
She's surely here, in the midst of her vassals and all of her tributaries. Let the Admiral Geminus assign them the agreed on place and when they have anchored, let me be told! Go!

(Anthony steps away from Octavia and Octavia alone can be seen by Cleopatra.)

CLEOPATRA (to herself)
Ah, messenger from hell! You were lying! She is beautiful!

(The curtains in the back are closed. During the action the day wanes, little by little. Cleopatra listens from the bed at first. Then, she gives up her hiding place without betraying herself and listens to the words and gestures of Octavia and Anthony. And, after a moment finds herself quite near them. Then, discouraged by what she hears and sees, she returns to the bed where she sits, overwhelmed, weeping.)

ANTHONY (to Octavia)
Your brother won't be the least surprised of all.

OCTAVIA (seated near the table)
Would to the gods these ships had never arrived.

ANTHONY (standing near her)
Why's that?

OCTAVIA
These reinforcements will make you bolder, less amenable to the advice of those who love you.

ANTHONY (seated near her)
Have I ever been rebellious towards you?

OCTAVIA (tenderly)
No. Except when it is a question of my brother.

ANTHONY (laughing)
Defend him if you dare!

OCTAVIA
Can I forget that, thanks to him, I am yours wife?

(Anthony crosses his hands holding Octavia's hands. He kisses her fingers as he speaks.)

ANTHONY
It's the only good thing he has done. And I have pardoned him many outrages in memory of the joy I owe him.

OCTAVIA
Since this joy still lasts, continue to pardon him.

ANTHONY
All patience has its limits. Moreover, I think it is precisely this happiness which exasperates him.

OCTAVIA (protesting)
Oh!

ANTHONY
Ah! yes! Doubtless he had other hopes in giving you to me.

OCTAVIA
What was it?

ANTHONY
That I would be a very bad husband to you.

OCTAVIA
You, so fine!

ANTHONY
What an admirable pretext to urge on his venomous agents! Himself shouting "Ah, citizens, you wanted this marriage? You see now, how Anthony, by the way he treats my sister, outrages the wife chosen for him by the Roman people."

OCTAVIA
He has never said such a thing.

ANTHONY
Because I have never given him the opportunity. But, all that can irritate a man and push him to extremes hasn't he coldly attempted? He owes me half of the fleet of Sextus Pompey—sixty triremes. He kept them. He owes me half of Sicily conquered from the pirates. He keeps it all. I had the right, after Lepidus was deposed, to my share of his provinces, his legions, his vassals, his treasures. He kept everything, clever man, distributing to his soldiers the Italian lands, and nothing to Anthony's soldiers. And his reply to my remonstrances—you know it! The most disdainful silence. Ah, dear sweet child, if I lose it without rage, it's for you and you alone.

OCTAVIA
I know it, and it's one of the reasons I love you. But, be patient still. I beg you for me—always for me.

ANTHONY (gaily)
Yes, for sure. And two armies will be there, arms in hand, waiting while Octavian regulates the fate of Rome.

OCTAVIA
Ah, gods! If I could regulate the fate of Rome it wouldn't take long—all the world would embrace—as we do. (she hugs him, Cleopatra reacts) But, it's in vain for me to pray—to conjure. They always treat me like a child. It's really true, too, that I understand nothing of your disputes. When I listen to Octavian, it seems to me he's right.

ANTHONY
Oh, for God's sake.

OCTAVIA (excitedly)
But, after you speak—he's in the wrong.

ANTHONY
Right.

OCTAVIA
Or rather, I think you are both wrong.

ANTHONY (laughing)
Ah, indeed.

OCTAVIA
Ah! Yes! You lend your ear to a crowd of ambitious, jealous, spiteful men, interested only in betraying you—instead of listening to those who love you both and who look only to your mutual benefit. Look, my adored Anthony! Look a little at my position, between this brother I love so much, and this husband who is dearer to me still—obliged if this war breaks out, to make vows for both parties at once. The gods will laugh at my prayers when I say to them, "Oh, immortals, protect my brother and my husband, too."

ANTHONY
They will abstain.

OCTAVIA
Fine, but there will always be a victor—and be it you or he—I will only weep over it.

ANTHONY
Make him recognize his mistakes.

OCTAVIA
Let me, at least, have time to try it! Give me the joy of disarming your hate through the strength of love. Alas, it is not enough that I have been able to succeed all alone, and that to convince you to do what I wanted—it required the presence of this fleet.

(Octavia lowers her voice.)

ANTHONY
What thought is concealed by your words?

OCTAVIA
Haven't you understood?

ANTHONY
I am not sure. Let's see. Look me carefully in the eyes.
(Anthony pulls Octavia to his lap. A more obvious reaction of rage by Cleopatra, who finds herself quite near and behind them.)

OCTAVIA
No, spare me this annoyance.

ANTHONY
Come on! Say it quietly. I am not looking at you, you see. (head on her shoulder) This fleet?

OCTAVIA
Where did it come from?

ANTHONY
From Alexandria.

OCTAVIA
And, by whose order?

ANTHONY
By order of the Queen of Egypt.

OCTAVIA
Ah! She sent it to you.

ANTHONY (smiling)
Come on, say it. You think the Queen of Egypt is there?

OCTAVIA
And, if she were?

ANTHONY
Are you jealous of her?

OCTAVIA (all the while in his arms, in a low voice)
Sometimes! Where I see you distracted and dreaming, I say to myself, "Perhaps he's thinking of her."

ANTHONY (embarrassed)
Child!

OCTAVIA
She is so powerful—even from afar! They say she's a sorceress.

ANTHONY
And, I willingly believe it; but rather she should be jealous of you. Your radiant youth, the innocent charm of your chaste bearing, your limpid eyes, they are your enchantments—more powerful than hers. Let her come and compare herself to you! She will sense that she's conquered and flee like a phantom of the right before the look of dawn.

(Cleopatra, torn apart, falls on the bed weeping.)

OCTAVIA
Yes, tell me that! Tell me especially that you love me. That word is enough.

ANTHONY
You still doubt it?

OCTAVIA
No.

ANTHONY
Will you stop doubting if I grant what you asked me just now?

OCTAVIA
You permit me to go find Octavian?

ANTHONY
Yes. These reinforcements which have joined me give me the right.

OCTAVIA
Do they?

ANTHONY
Let him give me, above all, my share of Pompey's fleet.

OCTAVIA
And then?

ANTHONY
And then, as to the rest, we will have new discussions. My friends and his will establish the basis of an alliance which I hope will last.

OCTAVIA
Oh, I'll answer for that!

ANTHONY (smiling, low)
Go! And let me send this fleet back to Egypt.

OCTAVIA
Ah! How I love you.

(Octavia jumps on Anthony's neck. The curtain rises. Demetrius, Dercetas, Thryseus, and Dellius enter.)

DELLIUS
The fleet has doubled the promontory.

ANTHONY
You come promptly. I was about to call you. My dearly beloved Octavia is going to propose an accommodation to Octavian.

THRYSEUS
Ah?

DERCETAS
Thanks be given to her.

ANTHONY (to Octavia)
Dellius will escort you to your brother. (to Dellius) See to it the escort be worthy of Anthony's wife—and that torch bearers precede and follow her litter.

OCTAVIA
And, before my return, you will not permit any act which resembles a provocation?

ANTHONY
I swear it to you. My soldiers will not take their arms, you know until they see the wooden pyres lit on the heights. They won't be lit unless I give the signal by lighting this one here. (pointing to it) Surrounded by our standards. I will give that signal when you return to tell me, "Octavian refuses."

OCTAVIA
Octavian will accept and these horrible pyres will not be lit.

DERCETAS
Please the immortal gods!

OCTAVIA
Let's go! Goodbye.

ANTHONY
Goodbye, sweet messenger! Go—and return to us with an olive branch in your hand.

OCTAVIA
I will answer for that.

(Octavia leaves.)

ANTHONY
Go, my soul follows you.

DERCETAS
And our prayers!

(They leave with her. Cleopatra is alone for a moment.)

CLEOPATRA
What more can he do to you? Wretch! Will you wait for him to kick you out? Go! Leave this place to the irreproachable spouse? Go on! Go! You have nothing more to do here. (at this moment Anthony reappears with his friends) Too late!

(Cleopatra hides behind the bed curtains. At the same time that Anthony and his friends return Strepsiades bearing papyrus scrolls and a Slave places a lamp on the table.)

ANTHONY
This is the map of the coast?

STREPSIADES
Yes, master.

ANTHONY
Place it on the table. (Slave obeys and retires) Well, friends. Are you satisfied, I think? Our affairs are on the way to an accommodation.

DEMETRIUS
So much the better! For war between you and Octavian would be like the earth opening and filling the gulf with bodies.

THRYSEUS
In your place, I would send the fleet back—right away.

ANTHONY (jesting)
To reassure Octavian?

THRYSEUS
To please our Romans and to hasten the conclusion of the peace, by proving to them there is nothing between this Queen and you.

ANTHONY
Are the rancors of the Forums so tenacious? Won't they ever pardon me the time lost in the delights of Alexandria?

DERCETAS
What they won't pardon you for, Mark Anthony, is for maintaining the Queen on her throne instead of converting Egypt into a Roman province.

DEMETRIUS
But, there is still time! Do it!

ANTHONY
Bah! Dispossess a woman who sent her fleet at my first call?

DERCETAS
Fine! She deserves nothing for doing what she had to.

DEMETRIUS
Her fate depends on you.

THRYSEUS
She is lost if you succumb.

ANTHONY
So be it. But, I cannot forget she loved me, and that, perhaps, she loves me still. Why smile?

THRYSEUS
It's not likely her love has survived your marriage to Octavia.

DERCETAS
I would think rather of her hate.

(As before, Cleopatra has lost nothing of this, listening with indignation at first, then rage, finally with a joy which clears and transforms her face as Anthony's jealousy and passion are revealed.)

ANTHONY
No matter! One must always be grateful to a woman who has given you pleasure.

THRYSEUS
What heart!

ANTHONY
Don't go believing that my indulgence is left over form my mad passion. Ah, great gods! All this is, indeed, far away. I am forever cured of her spells and what a deliverance.

DERCETAS
Ah, yes!

ANTHONY (gaily)
For you, too, right? Come, comrades, don't bite your lips. We are no longer in Memphis. Speak frankly. Admit that this break has filled you with joy.

ALL (with one voice)
Surely.

ANTHONY (laughing)
By Pollux! That's frankness!

THRYSEUS
Besides, there's no reason to lament over the fate of the beautiful lady. She is a woman who will gallantly take her part. She didn't weep long over Caesar.

ANTHONY (excitedly)
No, but to tell the truth, she never loved him. And then—she wasn't of an age to mummify herself in an eternal widowhood.

THRYSEUS
Right. But, decidedly, she shouldn't have so quickly given him a successor.

ANTHONY (shocked)
Me?

THRYSEUS
Oh, no! Not you. Before you, much before.

ANTHONY
Another! Ah! Bah! (laughing with a secret scorn) You see how they abuse her. I, who believed myself naively the only heir of Caesar! You must break with a woman to learn everything. (in a detached tone) And, who is this other person?

DEMETRIUS (excitedly)
Thryseus is going a bit far.

DERCETAS
Yes, perhaps it is a slander.

ANTHONY (laughing with a false gaiety)
And, why not the truth? Another? But, this is, indeed, rather funny. Come on! Thryseus, I am curious to know who it was? Let's see. Wasn't Cneius Pompey spoken of?

THRYSEUS
Oh, him, too.

ANTHONY (standing)
Also? Cneius?

THRYSEUS
He is not to be doubted!

ANTHONY
She denied it to me very forcefully.

THRYSEUS
Naturally. Cneius is dead. It was impossible for him to contradict her. A woman never admits to her lovers any but those that are incontestable—by whom she could be betrayed. And, when she admits three—you may boldly suppose ten.

ANTHONY
You should have heard her deny it! "Cneius, this fool—this—Sextus—pass over him. He was a man at least! But, his brother—What kind of idea do you have of me?"

THRYSEUS
Yes, yes. We know this feminine way of arguing.

ANTHONY
She was, perhaps, in good faith. (all look at him) Eh! Yes. (ironic) She must have forgotten about him.

(General laughter.)

THRYSEUS
Ah! Ah! Charming! Charming!

ANTHONY (sitting down again)
It's an admirable thing. The ease with which a woman forgets her old lovers. (bitterly) Unfortunately, she alone forgets them.

THRYSEUS
No one ever said anything more just.

ANTHONY (continuing to pretend indifference)
So, after Caesar, Cneius. And another one. But, who? Who were you speaking of first?

THRYSEUS
Herod?

ANTHONY
The Jew? The little King of Judea?

THRYSEUS
Himself.

ANTHONY
Is it possible? Just gods! That one is, indeed, the last I would have suspected. Herod! (breaks out laughing) This bad abortion of a king, sulky, fearful, who always goes hugging the walls. Ah! Ah! That's a true clown.

DEMETRIUS
We see, with pleasure, that you take it as a joke.

ANTHONY (raging)
And how else to take it? Herod! That insect that I would squash with two fingers—it's to die laughing.

THRYSEUS (laughing)
The fact is—

ANTHONY
Herod! After him, one could believe anything. And yourself, Thryseus, who knows—

(Laughter.)

THRYSEUS (protesting, modestly)
No!

ANTHONY
Bah! Don't defend yourself! Admit it. Come on, admit it!

THE OTHERS (joking)
Admit it, Thryseus.

THRYSEUS (seriously)
No, truly! There was never anything between her and me.

ANTHONY (sickened)
That's how he protects himself. Seriously, the coward. How could such a thing be possible? And, he's right! Why not? Good gods. On what basis are we to suppose that these creatures respect themselves, any more than my hunting bitches. Yet, I am astonished that no one except you has mentioned Herod to me! (standing, with a restrained rage) All you should have done, day and night, was to yell in my ears, "Herod, Herod, Herod!" Disgust would have cured me of my stupid passion.

DEMETRIUS
How would anyone suppose you to be unaware of a fact known to all the children of Alexandria?

ANTHONY
Eh! By Hercules! Isn't he who is most interested always the one who knows nothing?

THRYSEUS
And then, in sum, all this is past which you cannot ask her to account about.

ANTHONY
Yes! Another fine argument of their inventory, "I didn't love you then." In short, I have supped at the same table as all these other men. What a feast! Let's talk of something else. Do you think this woman will be with her fleet?

DEMETRIUS
It's not likely.

ANTHONY
Why?

DEMETRIUS
She would have told you by the same man who announced the arrival of her ships.

ANTHONY
Then, so much the better! I won't have to pray her to stay on her gallery and spare me the honor of her person. Do you know who commands her fleet?

THRYSEUS
Who do you expect it to be, if not the inevitable, indispensable Kephren?

ANTHONY
Kephren.

THRYSEUS
Doubtless. Since our departure from Memphis, Kephren has taken on the authority of a master. The Queen has made him chief of the Royal Council, Minister of the Palace, Disburser of Benefits and Graces, Commander of all troops on land and sea.

ANTHONY
And, to what does he owe these favors?

THRYSEUS
Ah! The women!

ANTHONY (jumping)
What?

THRYSEUS (vivaciously)
But, as to him, you have nothing to say! He has succeeded you.

(Cleopatra is about to hurl herself on Thryseus and stab him, but she is prevented by Anthony, who more promptly seizes Thryseus by the throat. From this moment, Cleopatra, reassured, changes her attitude.)

ANTHONY (beside himself)
Wretch! You lie! You lie! Say that you are lying.

THRYSEUS (stretched on his seat)
Ah! Mercy!

(ANTHONY's friends interpose.)

ANTHONY
Let me alone! This clown is saying things which one can no longer believe.

DEMETRIUS, DERCETAS
Come on! Come on! Mark Anthony!

(Demetrius and Dercetas free Thryseus.)

ANTHONY
A valet! This rogue dares to say that a valet—

THRYSEUS (readjusting himself and breathing)
Ask Demetrius if I have invented anything.

ANTHONY
He persists?

DEMETRIUS
Easy! Nothing will clear up with rage. But, you see us, indeed, surprised! Where is this fury coming from? And, what does it matter to you today, whatever is happening between her and Kephren?

ANTHONY
Come! It's a shame and I don't wish it said that a woman I loved would give herself to a valet! It's humiliating to me.

DEMETRIUS
A poor reason, you will agree, and which makes you seem less cured than you pretend.

ANTHONY
Oh, as to cured, I am, indeed. But, why wound me with these ridiculous rumors? Kephren? It's stupid, you see. Admit that it is stupid.

DEMETRIUS
Someone surprised them.

ANTHONY
Slander!

DERCETAS
One of your messengers, Trasillus, was introduced to the Queen's chamber and found them together asleep.

DEMETRIUS
And, Kephren, awakened with a leap and three-quarters strangled him.

ANTHONY
Enough! Enough! Shut up! In his arms. This valet!

DEMETRIUS
But, still, one more time—what does it matter to you at this time?

ANTHONY
Ah! What's it matter to me? It matters to us all! Picture then, a creature capable of lying, of betraying with so much impudence, who assures us, if there is a battle, that at the height of the battle, she won't go over to Octavian with all her fleet commanded by her Kephren?

THRYSEUS (quickly)
Then, it would be better to send that fleet away.

ANTHONY
She couldn't betray more quickly.

DEMETRIUS
Let us fight on land!

DERCETAS
It's the wish of all our soldiers, who feel ill at ease on these triremes.

ANTHONY (striding back and forth)
Yes, yes, I know it. Night! In the arms of that man. Prostituted!

DERCETAS
Besides, will we come to blows?

DEMETRIUS
At present, it's very unlikely!

ANTHONY (still following his idea)
Is it unlikely?

DEMETRIUS and DERCETAS (surprised)
Doubtless.

ANTHONY
Why? He is young, he is handsome, that man. He is completely devoted to her. He is always near her. Which gave him the opportunity. And with women—opportunity is everything.

(Demetrius and Dercetas look at each other in consternation. Thryseus laughs behind his cape. Cleopatra, reassured, plays with the golden mirror.)

DERCETAS
Excuse us, we were speaking of Octavian.

ANTHONY (exploding)
And I, I am speaking of this infamous Queen and her ignoble lover! Let's see her! I wish to see her.

DERCETAS
You want to—?

ANTHONY
I want to see her! Go to her galley and let her be brought to me. Right now!

DEMETRIUS
But, if she refuses?

ANTHONY
Go on! You will see her come—the impudent one, smiling with her eyes, lies on her lips and you will hear her plead her defense. And this Kephren, too. Let him be brought here, too, that one. The beloved Kephren. We will congratulate him.

DEMETRIUS
What are you thinking, master? And what will you do with them in your camp?

ANTHONY
Hostages for our safety if there is a fight. And, if there is a peace signed, we will strangle them before the entire army—the perjured Queen and her accomplice—chained to one another.

THRYSEUS
And the entire camp will applaud!

ANTHONY
Go! And if you value your life, don't tell me she won't come.

CLEOPATRA (parting the curtain)
That would be a lie.

(Stupor. Silence. A movement of surprise by all. Anthony takes the lamp on the table and raising the lamp, goes to the bed and assures himself it is, indeed, Cleopatra.)

ANTHONY (to his friends)
Leave us!

(They leave, silently, by the rear. The curtains fall, closing the bay.)

ANTHONY (putting the lamp back)
Ah, you were there.

CLEOPATRA
I wanted to see. I've seen. I wanted to know. I know.

ANTHONY
And, what do you know?

CLEOPATRA
In what way Cleopatra is spoken of here!

ANTHONY
Yes, yes, insidious creature! Hurry to avoid the storm. Shall we say a word about this Kephren?

CLEOPATRA
Not before having said two words about this Octavia.

ANTHONY
It's your excuse, this political marriage imposed by the health of my situation—and that was exacted from me by all the Roman people?

CLEOPATRA
Really? It was only to please the Roman people, what just now passed between you and her, and the roses from her belt, spilled on this bedcover! Politics, pure politics?

ANTHONY
Ah! Serpent of the Nile! You knew, indeed, that love was for nothing, and you are not the woman to misunderstand it, knowing more about it than Anthony. But, you! You! Dare you say what an ignoble passion threw you into the arms of Kephren!

CLEOPATRA
What do you know about it?

ANTHONY
Ah! You don't admit it, that one?

CLEOPATRA
What do you care?

ANTHONY
Look, is he your lover—yes or no?

CLEOPATRA
And, why not? (movement by Anthony) He is valiant, devoted, faithful.

ANTHONY (ironically)
And, especially handsome, right? Beauty is not to be disdained in a man?

CLEOPATRA
No more than in a woman! Witness Octavia, of whom I make you compliment! She has something to charm all eyes.

ANTHONY
Always Octavia! A fine pretext not to reply and to spare you the shame of an admission.

CLEOPATRA
And what admission do I owe you! It's very nice, truly. This man who left me, swearing of his love to men and gods! And the first chance, arriving in Rome he marries another! Who disowns me, who insults me before his friends, his wife, the entire world. And who dares, after all this, to ask me to account for how I employ my widowhood! And, if it were true, coward. That from rage, despair and a spirit of revenge and to be as you, I had taken this man for lover! To whose fault, if not the betrayer who gave me the example of betrayal.

ANTHONY (beside himself)
Is it true, then? You admit it, then? Is it really true?

CLEOPATRA
True or not, do I owe you an explanation? Do you alone have the privilege of betraying your sworn oath? You marry whom you wish. I love whoever pleases me! Come on, you are beside the point, Mark Anthony, you still think you are in Memphis. Here we are, not two lovers, nor even two friends! But two allies! Nothing more! You cannot win without my help, I will no longer be Queen without your support. Let us accept the forced union which interest imposes on us. Let us speak of our common well being, of Queen to Triumvir— as statesmen. And, let us leave these useless quarrels, for a past which has no longer any right except to be forgotten.

ANTHONY
Ah, you forget it, you! I, never! After a love such as ours, it is not forgotten; it turns to hate.

CLEOPATRA
So be it! Let us hate each other, then! But, let us be victorious, the one through the other. You have in this roadstead a fleet that has no equal in the world. What orders do you give me for tonight?

ANTHONY
Ah, I am, indeed, thinking of that!

CLEOPATRA
And, of what, then?

ANTHONY (with brutal passion)
Of you!

CLEOPATRA
Say, rather of Octavia, who is going to bring you in the folds of her skirt, either peace or war. I understand, moreover, that you will decide nothing before her return. Let us wait until tomorrow. For tonight, we have said everything. (rises) I think—see, night is falling. I will retire.

ANTHONY
And, where are you going to spend the night?

CLEOPATRA
Aboard my galley, the *Antonian*.

ANTHONY
Where Kephren awaits you?

CLEOPATRA
Doubtless! He is in command.

ANTHONY (violently)
And, I, I forbid you to go find this man.

CLEOPATRA
You forbid me?

ANTHONY
Yes.

CLEOPATRA
By what right?

ANTHONY
By right of my hate for him and you! Yes, my hate! Yes, I hate you, sorceress, who have so well mixed your poisons into my flesh and in my soul that I can no longer tear you out! Ah, cursed one! Far from your enchantments I could breathe. I thought myself freed and forever escaped from your fatal love. But, there you are, with that voice which bewitches me, with looks that burn me. It's useless for me to struggle, to argue with myself, to repeat to myself with rage all that compels me to flee you. To yell to myself, "It's over! I no longer love her! I execrate her! I scorn her. This infamous Queen who gives herself to her servant." The more I insult you, the more I feel your sorceress' charm which twists me and wounds my heart, and I will only escape it's pull by killing you, you and your Kephren—for I will kill him, understand that clearly—before your eyes, your ignoble lover! I will kill him!

CLEOPATRA (sitting down and watching him, all the while with a triumphant smile)
Yes! Yes. That will be very fine! And, also, the desire, the mad desire to kill! Good! There you are, just as I wanted you. (standing, triumphant) Enough, enough! You are suffering in your turn. And you are then, you too, well tortured, quite enraged by this force of jealousy! Now you have for your part all that I have endured from you! For so many days and nights! Now you know the despair—powerless to do what may not be. Ah, wretch! There, before my

eyes—a woman! Another, in your arms. And, from this bed, still hot from your embraces, everything can be seen and understood! I don't rejoice in twisting the iron in your heart, as you did in mine, executioner! You are suffering, right? Say it, say that you are, indeed, in pain! Say that my lust, my betrayal desolates you! Say it. Say it, so I can savor slowly the misery which tears you apart, which punishes you, and which avenges me!

ANTHONY
Well, you are avenged. So be it! You weren't with this man only to punish my betrayal, as you call it—without love; your head was lost, madly—and I feel myself capable of forgetting this momentary vertigo, and of pardoning, and—

CLEOPATRA (quickly)
Be careful. Your wife will hear you!

ANTHONY
Never mind that child who deserves a better fate. I honestly constrained myself to love her to drive your image out with hers! Madness! Never—never for a single day was I freed from the obsession of your memory! Even in her arms, it haunts me. I look at her, it's you that I see. She speaks to me—it's you I hear. And, even in the kisses I give her, it's not you that I betray with her—it's she I betray for you! Her icy love breaks at the thought of our burning desire like snow in the light of the sun. And the sun of my life is you! You are my vision, my heart, my strength. You appear, and I leave a long dolor. My choked senses reanimate, my sleeping heart awakes. My blood throbs more alert and hot in my veins. Sorceress, perhaps! Sorceress, so be it! And, what does it matter to me? If you are with me, by what enchantments you madden me, and by what spells? I adore you.

CLEOPATRA
Even guilt?

ANTHONY
Even guilt.

CLEOPATRA
Despite Kephren?

ANTHONY
In spite of him! In spite of all!

CLEOPATRA
Ah. For this cry of love! I pardon you! And I abrogate your penance which should last longer.

ANTHONY
What?

CLEOPATRA
Senseless one, who believed me capable of this infamy! There's only one traitor here! You! And Kephren is nothing to me, you understand, except a faithful servant whose lips have never touched anything but the dust of my sandals.

ANTHONY
Ah! If I could believe it! But you are lying.

CLEOPATRA
I am lying?

ANTHONY
Yes, yes, you are lying! And to what good? Him dead, all would be said.

CLEOPATRA
You don't believe me!

ANTHONY
Come on! This man that you have made the first in the realm after you! That they surprised one night in your arms!

CLEOPATRA
But, it's false! It's false! It's false! He was sleeping at the sill of my door like a faithful dog guarding your possession.

ANTHONY
Ah, prove that, then.

CLEOPATRA
And how can I prove it to you?

ANTHONY
You can do it!

CLEOPATRA
But, how? Say how?

ANTHONY
How? I would go kill him!

CLEOPATRA
Yes!

ANTHONY (taking her hand and looking her carefully in the eyes)
Kill him yourself!

CLEOPATRA
I?

ANTHONY
Here, by your hand, under my eyes.

CLEOPATRA
I, how can I?

ANTHONY
Ah! You hesitate! You see—you tremble for him!

CLEOPATRA
I pity him! It's a bad reward for his devotion! But, if it must be done?

ANTHONY
It must be done!

CLEOPATRA
At least, at this price, you would believe me?

ANTHONY
At this price only.

CLEOPATRA
Then, let it be as you wish. I am ready. (Anthony takes the dagger on the bed and presents it to her) No need! I have better. This blow and Olympus' poison, we will try on the unfortunate. Let him come!

ANTHONY
Where is he?

CLEOPATRA
At the door, where he followed me.

ANTHONY
Naturally.

(Anthony goes and calls, raising the curtain. Cleopatra pours wine in the cup.)

ANTHONY
Kephren. (coming back) Your mistress calls you.

CLEOPATRA
Come here, Kephren! Do you know what crime you are guilty of towards me?

KEPHREN
I, mistress?

CLEOPATRA
You, who have furnished weapons to slander by your foolish passion for your mistress.

KEPHREN (falling to his knees)
O, Mistress! Who has dared to say to you what your humble slave dares hardly to admit to himself?

CLEOPATRA
Your looks have spoken for you! And the evil watchers don't hold you alone culpable.

KEPHREN
Powerful gods! They haven't dared.

CLEOPATRA
To say I am your accomplice. Yes! And, Mark Anthony doesn't doubt it.

KEPHREN
Infamy! You, you! Ah, how to dissolve your rage and merit your pardon.

CLEOPATRA
There is no mercy for a slave who dares look on his mistress. Are you ready for all the punishments to expiate your crime?

KEPHREN (groveling)
O Queen, you can ask? For all! Even death!

CLEOPATRA (throwing in the cup the pearl from her purse)
Here it is! From my hand! Drink and prove to the Triumvir that you are no more to my eyes than the drop of water from the Nile and a grain of sand from the desert.

(Cleopatra gives him the cup.)

KEPHREN (taking the cup)
Let the immortals add to your existence the days taken from mine.

(starts to drink)

ANTHONY (tearing the cup from his hands)
Stop! Unfortunate fellow!

(Anthony throws the cup away.)

ANTHONY (to Cleopatra)
It's enough to justify you both. And his death would spoil my happiness. (amorously seizes the hands of Cleopatra and draws her into his arms joyously) Go, Kephren, loyal and faithful friend. Go, sleep in peace. Go!

CLEOPATRA (still in Anthony's arms)
And have the ship advance. We are leaving.

(Kephren leaves.)

ANTHONY (still holding Cleopatra's hands)
Leaving?

CLEOPATRA
Doubtless!

ANTHONY
Go, then! Are we to separate again? When you are here, justified, innocent, adored—to tear yourself from my arms? (holding her tightly) Well, try!

CLEOPATRA
And Octavia?

ANTHONY
Forget about Octavia! I have you, and hold you. I keep you and you won't leave me any more.

CLEOPATRA
But, she's coming! See the torches at the bridge on the other river. It's she. She's here!

ANTHONY
Let her come!

CLEOPATRA (pulling away)
What, then? And, I am going to wait for her, right? To be a witness again to your embraces? (Anthony tries to pull her back, but She releases herself) Come! Are you thinking or have you conceived the monstrous dream of not separating from your spouse and renewing things with your mistress?

ANTHONY
No!

CLEOPATRA
Then, let's finish. Time presses. It is not agreeable to me to find myself on the sill of your door with the woman who has stolen your love from me. One of us two is too many. Make your choice and make it quickly. She or I!

ANTHONY
You, you alone, and always you!

CLEOPATRA
And, if she comes?

ANTHONY
She won't come!

CLEOPATRA
And, how will you prevent her?

ANTHONY
By tearing down the bridge!

CLEOPATRA
Weigh carefully what you are going to do, Triumvir! She is your wife, humiliated, repudiated, chased out!

ANTHONY
For always.

CLEOPATRA
That's war!

ANTHONY
Go for war!

CLEOPATRA
And the fire put to this pyre, it's the burning of the world.

ANTHONY
Let the world burn! And let its furnace light our love! Torch these pyres and let the wind spread the fire. Sound the trumpets and let the wind carry their clarion call. It pleases me that war empurples you with its light and salutes you with its fanfare. Tomorrow, in your honor, the first battle.

CLEOPATRA
On the sea!

ANTHONY
You prefer it?

CLEOPATRA
For, henceforth, I can no longer count on the pity of Octavian! Captive, I am dead! On my galley, at least, in case of disaster, I will escape him!

ANTHONY
So be it then! For you, we will triumph on the sea!

CLEOPATRA
Then, hurry! For Octavian has already gone halfway.

ANTHONY (at the rear, in a thunderous voice)
Destroy the bridge!

CLEOPATRA (triumphant)
Now! I have him!

(The curtains open and the shore can be seen full of soldiers.)

DEMETRIUS (on the sill, to Mark Anthony)
But, Octavia is there.

DERCETAS
She's coming.

ANTHONY (coming forward, followed by Kephren, Demetrius, Dercetas, Thryseus, Juba, etc.) There is no more of Octavia!

(His friends express alarm.)

DEMETRIUS
And, if she's bringing us peace?

ANTHONY
All the more reason! Negotiate when we have the advantage of strength to recommence hostilities in six months? That would be a stupidity.

(Approbation by his friends.)

GROUP OF OFFICERS
Yes! Yes! Mark Anthony's right! War!

(The lictors take their fasces from the foot of the pyre and the officers their standards.)

DEMETRIUS
So be it! Then, let us fight!

ANTHONY
At sea! Where we have four vessels to one to put on line—thanks to the most powerful of our allies. (turns to Cleopatra) The most faithful of our friends. (looks at Thryseus, Demetrius and Decetas who do not flinch) And, by her fleet, commanded by the loyal and valiant Kephren! (puts his hand on the shoulder of Kephren amicably)

THRYSEUS (aside)
You struggle then against this woman?

ANTHONY (to Juba who reappears)
Well—the bridge?

JUBA
Destroyed, master.

ANTHONY
Now, to the pyre! Let the entire army know that the truce is broken. Give me that torch

CLEOPATRA
I'll do it, if you like, Triumvir! Let Cleopatra have the joy of lighting the first fire of your discord.

ANTHONY
Go, then! (Cleopatra takes the torch) And, tomorrow—the battle! And, in a month, to Rome.

ALL
Yes! Yes! To Rome! To Rome!

CLEOPATRA (alone, aside, torch in hand)
Rome is Octavia! You won't enter there—in Rome.

(Cleopatra goes up between the soldiers who acclaim her and lights the pyre.)

ALL (shouting and striking their shields)
Glory to Mark Anthony and Cleopatra. Victory to the Triumvir! To Rome! To Rome!

(The pyre catches fire, blazes up and shows Cleopatra and the entire roadstead with a blood red light, and the trophy, hidden by the fasces, appears, standing and all the officers carrying standards, grouped around Cleopatra, and all the soldiers shaking their weapons.)

CURTAIN

ACT V

Scene 5

Alexandria

The palace of Cleopatra, where a peristyle links the palace to the Temple of Isis. Beyond the peristyle, which supports a cedar ceiling, the gardens planted with palms, dates, mimosa, tamarind, and acacia, along with cypresses and sycamores. At the extremity of the gardens a terrace which dominates Alexandria, quite red under the sun and where one can see the cupola of the Serapion and the white tower of the Pharos.

Olympus, leaning on a column of the peristyle and a group of slaves, overseers, guards, and officers, listening uneasily to the rumors which rise from the city. Suddenly these voices are mixed with trumpet calls.

AN OFFICER
Listen! The call to arms!

OTHERS
What! The ships announced are hardly in port.

OVERSEER
Listen.

(The Diviner, Satiris, appears on the sill of the temple to the left.)

DIVINER
What's the meaning of this tumult in the Gardens of the Queen? And these breathless trumpets which trouble even the priests in the sanctuaries of our gods?

OLYMPUS
The fleet has returned.

DIVINER
Already? The expected battle has not taken place?

OLYMPUS
Or the fleet is coming to seek reinforcements?

OVERSEER (coming forward)
We can only wait to learn.

OLYMPUS
Then, even you have sent for news?

OVERSEER
No one has returned.

OLYMPUS
Send others. (on an order from the Overseer, the same slaves hastily leave) Ah, why don't I follow them? Alas, the greater the weight of years, the more the sun burns—the anguish breaks my knees.

(An overseer comes forward with a slave who has just arrived. All come forward and surround him.)

OVERSEER
The Queen has just arrived at the palace.

(Movement.)

OLYMPUS (with a step toward the palace)
Already! We will know from her.

OVERSEER (stopping him)
You will learn nothing. The Queen has shut herself up. It is forbidden to trouble her repose.

OLYMPUS
Must one think there's been a defeat?

DIVINER
Does Mark Anthony accompany the Queen?

OVERSEER
No. The Queen's ships have an hour's start of him and Mark Anthony hasn't yet arrived in the port.

GUARD (who comes running in)
He's taking shelter now, he's arraying his galleys, after having shut behind him the passage from the Arsenal by extra heavy chains.

DIVINER
Is he maneuvering to attract Octavian?

OLYMPUS
Or, already defeated, does he fear to be followed even here?

(New trumpet sounds.)

SLAVE (who runs in, very troubled)
Misfortune for us! The Roman fleet is come!

(Movement.)

OLYMPUS
Powerful gods!

THRYSEUS (entering shortly afterward)
Ah, yes, that of Octavian. Enlarged by ships he has taken from Mark Anthony.

(Movement, rumors.)

DIVINER
What do you say?

(Two guards and overseers are approaching.)

OLYMPUS
Thus, the defeat we feared?

THRYSEUS
The defeat is only too real. And, victorious Octavian has put himself in pursuit of Anthony. Before night, the Romans will have disembarked and Alexandria will be invested on all sides.

(Movement of terror and noise from all.)

OLYMPUS
Powerful gods! The city besieged.

DIVINER
May the sacred trinity protect us!

KEPHREN (runs in, in full armor)
Let's go! Archers to the ramparts!

(Distant trumpets. Sortie by soldiers.)

DERCETAS
What, already?

KEPHREN
The triumvirs of Octavian are coming alongside across from the cisterns of Rhakotis.

OLYMPUS
God!

KEPHREN
And the disembarking has commenced already. (to soldiers reentering) Go—to arms!

(They leave.)

DIVINER (quickly)
If you strip guards from the palace, who will guard the Queen?

KEPHREN
Her Egyptian guards of whom I am retaking command. (to officers) You will be in charge of the Necropolis gate, you of the Canopis gate, you of the Arsenal. The Greek mercenaries will suffice there. The Gauls will guard the precincts of Bruchium. As for the gate to the cisterns, there Romans are needed. Who will command them?

THRYSEUS
I will. It's a post of honor which I reclaim, as a friend of Anthony and in his name.

KEPHREN
So be it. Run to occupy it, and remember that it is you that Octavian will act against immediately.

THRYSEUS
He will find out who he is speaking to.

(Thryseus goes off in the distance. The Egyptian Officers have disappeared.)

KEPHREN (to Overseers)
You, see to it that the guard of the treasury is doubled and confided to trusted men. You, go tell the priests to put themselves to praying.

DIVINER
The priests are at the feet of the gods. Listen! (in the temple to the left the priests can be heard singing accompanied by harps) Horus! Isis! Osiris!

KEPHREN
May the gods hear them.

(The Overseers have gone off.)

OLYMPUS
But still, how did we get here? And with her own fleet, that of the Queen, that of the tributary states. Why wasn't the valiant triumvir victorious?

KEPHREN
Victory was assured. His heavy ships, seeming like floating citadels commenced a maneuver that the Egyptian fleet ought to have followed. The order came from the galley *Antonian* where Cleopatra was stationed; our vessels waited only for a signal to enter the line. I prayed the Queen twice to give this signal. She seemed not to understand me. "Queen," I said again, "the hour is decisive! Anthony is outflanking Octavian and will destroy him. Finish his work. Assure his triumph. Command. Attack." "His triumph," she murmured. Then she came to the prow, under the eyes of all our sailors, and in a terrible voice she ordered "Retreat."

DIVINER
What?

KEPHREN
"What are you doing," I cried. "Retreat—with full sails. Head for Egypt." The pilot obeyed, the oars reversed and then we were flee-

ing—and behind us, all the vessels of the Queen, and behind them all the vessels of the tributary states.

OLYMPUS
Merciful gods!

KEPHREN
Not a moment had the Queen taken her eyes from Anthony's ship. "Is he going to continue the struggle?" she said aloud. Anthony seemed resolved. His heavy triremes continued their maneuvers. The Queen had become very pale—and I heard her attempt a prayer. Then, suddenly interrupting herself: "See, Kephren. His triremes have stopped. They are turning their prows south. They deploy their sails. He is following us." And she smiled!

DIVINER (to Olympus)
Have the gods struck her with madness?

KEPHREN
The soldiers left on the shore of Actium watched us flee—lost. "Retreat," repeated the Queen. Octavian at first thought, suspected, it was a trick, then decided to pursue us, his light vessels quickly overtook our stragglers. The retreat became a route. From one galley to the next the tributaries began deserting. The first night, no more than fifty were behind us. The next night the number had been reduced to half. Thus the fleet dwindled hour by hour. You have seen the Queen arrive with the wreckage of ours. Anthony has just sheltered in the port with the remainder of his. Still, it was through my cares that the chains have been raised that stretch from the harbor to the Arsenal. Anthony wasn't thinking of that, so much has rage intoxicated him. Choking with rage, having to pursue her without reaching her. "Why do you speak to me of Octavian?" he raged, "and of his camp set up on the shore. The enemy is not on the shore—it's here." And, standing on the prow, he points to the palace, complaining of not being able to run there, accusing his friends of treason. "You delay the disembarking so as to give her time to escape my fury. You won't escape it, neither you nor she."

ANTHONY (in the gardens)
Leave me.

OLYMPUS
Listen!

ANTHONY (violently)
Where is she?

DIVINER (who has moved forward a step)
It's he! It's Mark Anthony!

OLYMPUS (seized)
Kephren! Save us from his rage!

KEPHREN
Thanks to the gods! The Queen is warned and guarded. Come! Come!

(Kephren rushes them into the palace and enters after them.)

DERCETAS (running in under the portico)
Mark Anthony!

ANTHONY (entering)
Where is she?

DEMETRIUS (entering)
Listen to me.

ANTHONY
Here she cannot escape. I have her!

(Demetrius bars the door to the palace with Dercetas and Juba.)

DEMETRIUS
Stop!

DERCETAS
What do you intend to do?

ANTHONY
I will shut that lying mouth, those perverse eyes. I will destroy this evil beast. I will strangle her while she is still hot with her crime. Let me go!

(Anthony wants to pass.)

DEMETRIUS
Wait, at least!

ANTHONY
What? So she can finish her work. So she can call to her aid the people of Alexandria and Octavian and hell? No! And, since the gods forget, give place to the descendant of Hercules to kill the monster.

(Anthony disengages himself violently and rushes towards the door of the palace.)

DEMETRIUS
Hercules wouldn't let her off so easily.

(Anthony stops short.)

DERCETAS
He would have pulled her from her lair and punished her before everyone.

ANTHONY (struck)
Before everyone! By heaven! Yes, that's what must be done. Before all! It's too little for her to die. Shame is due her!

DEMETRIUS
And there is still time if you don't want a revolt to break out.

DERCETAS
Already, we have trouble to contain our men.

ANTHONY (coming forward)
They are right! I owe them their vengeance. Yes, all those who saw her give the signal to break away—let them come! Go. And promise them a spectacle worthy of Actium. All those who shared in her outrage—all will watch her punishment.

DERCETAS
Right!

ANTHONY
And, bring in the people of Alexandria! Let them know how Romans pay back treason—

DEMETRIUS and DERCETAS
At once!

ANTHONY
Since Tarsus, where the sorceress overcame her judge, I owe you all a revenge. Mark Anthony is going to give her to you. Bring on the Lictors.

DEMETRIUS (to Dercetas, ready to leave)
Let's go.

ANTHONY
And, do it quickly, or my rage won't wait for your return.

(Demetrius, Dercetas and Juba leave. In the temple to the left, the priests repeat the invocation of the Egyptian trinity, "Horus! Osiris! Isis!")

ANTHONY
Ah, cowardly spy! You are afraid now! Seeing yourself lost, you cry in a moving plea to your gods. (coming to the temple, he pushes

open the door) No—only her priests in there. She is hiding in the depths of her palace.

CLEOPATRA (leaving the palace while the preceding occurs, under the portico) And, why should I hide myself?

ANTHONY (struck by her calm)
There she is! And haughty. By Hercules! She braves me! She doesn't tremble at my sight!

CLEOPATRA (coming to him)
And, why should I tremble at your sight?

ANTHONY (already near her, pulling his dagger, violently)
Because, I've got you now, wretched woman, much too satiated already to flee! You need to escape me at all costs, and take time to assure your well-being by delivering me to the conqueror. I admit you are occupied with it already, and that you both are negotiating over the price of that action.

CLEOPATRA (shrugging her shoulders)
You are demented.

ANTHONY
And, it is for this abject creature that I have lost the honor of my name. It's to this merchant of my honor that I sacrificed the love of Octavia. "Outrage, repudiate your wife and I am yours, faithful to death—on one condition, that you will fight at sea. Retreat will be easier." And treason, too, right?

CLEOPATRA (disdainfully)
Treason!

ANTHONY
Dare say your flight was not planned in advance and that you did not shout "Retreat" from a woman's weakness.

CLEOPATRA (coldly)
No, truly! Of what could I have been afraid? Of a wound? Where I was, the arrows could not reach me. Of defeat? I would have cried "Forward". Victory was certain.

ANTHONY (jumping)
Ah! You admit it, then?

CLEOPATRA
Yes, I admit it.

ANTHONY
And, voluntarily?

CLEOPATRA
And voluntarily I set sail for Egypt to bring you after me.

ANTHONY
And to steal victory from me!

CLEOPATRA
Yes, for this victory would be the ruin and defeat of our love.

ANTHONY
Its ruin? Senseless! I conquer. You would reenter Rome triumphantly with me!

CLEOPATRA
In your chariot, right? On one side, Cleopatra, and the other, Octavia.

ANTHONY
I repudiated her—Octavia! And you were the wife of the Dictator, of Caesar, the Master of the World.

CLEOPATRA
Yes, oh, yes, I know that language! I've been tricked by that already. It's word for word what the Divine Julius said to me after Pharsalus: "Come to Rome, O Queen. I will repudiate Calpurnia and you will be the wife of the Dictator, the Master of the World, of Caesar." And I followed the conqueror. Was he man enough to brave for me the rage of Roman men or the jealousy of Roman women? Humiliated, insulted, threatened, I had to return in shame to Egypt, giving place to the implacable matron! And I should have made the same mistake? Rome would once again have seen me at your side, putting up with rage more bitter, and outrages more bloody? Insanely, stupidly, I would have placed myself, as your glorious model had done. (Anthony reacts) Come, you would have done it, and more quickly still, for you are weaker than he was! To the caresses of your wife, to the advice of your friends, you would have sacrificed without remorse the Barbarian Queen, the enemy of the Roman people—the Egyptian charged with all sorts of crimes. And you would have driven me off, coward. For your Calpurnia is young and seductive, and you have already deceived me with her! Well, that's what I don't want—now—understand! No, you won't return to triumph in the Rome I hate. No, you won't see her in the first rank of women come to acclaim you, your Octavia, whom I execrate. Actium created between your chaste spouse and you, an abyss which nothing can bridge again. Better than seas, your disaster separates you, and without hope of repair. I would love you still better, defeated, proscribed, but completely mine, than hers, but victorious.

ANTHONY
O woman, woman, execrable woman! Listen to this, furies, it's worthy of you! She did nothing except from love of me!

CLEOPATRA
And, for who else?

ANTHONY
Ah, just gods. So many battles in the snows of the Alps—in the sands of the desert. So many cities taken. So many kings bowing

their scepters before my sword. So many honors and acclamations—to come to this. (falling into a seat, overwhelmed) Octavian, the vilest enemy, adroit only in underground maneuvers. It's the mole which triumphs over the lion! And because of the stupid egoism of a woman, my best ships captured, sunk, my legionnaires dispersed, captured or dead! On the shore of Actium, not a wave which doesn't roll up over a cadaver! And you have no horror of yourself, sorceress, at the thought of so many brave men dead, hopeless, cursing Mark Anthony, and that it is you, and you along, do you understand, you who have sacrificed them to mad chimeras of your stupid and ferocious jealousy?

CLEOPATRA
Ah, I really have time to count the dead! Ships are made to be sunk, and soldiers to be killed. Are we all powerful so we can stop these things? I was going to lose you; to chain you to me, more than a hecatomb was needed, and I would have sold them to flames and sold their blood; shame on you, if you are not a man, as you said to give half the world for Cleopatra! I am not boasting when I swear to you, that for you, I would destroy the universe! Big deal, truly, that there are some soldiers and sailors less in the world! What's important is that there remains for us, one more battle, which it's up to you to turn into a victory!

ANTHONY (bitterly, head in his hands)
A victory! Now!

CLEOPATRA
Come on, get up! And be Mark Anthony again.

ANTHONY
And, what battle? What possible victory? At least, by provoking this myrmidon to mortal combat, where alone we could struggle like two gladiators?

CLEOPATRA
Dreams! Instead of getting drunk on useless words, see where you have been led by my trick! And, thank Cleopatra for only delaying your triumph to offer it to you here, where it is more sure and brilliant.

ANTHONY (raising his head)
Here? You? Are you losing your wits?

CLEOPATRA
And you, have you at this troubled time, forgotten through your rage, your ability as a soldier? Eh! What? Great Captain. Do I have to teach you, that by following you in pursuit of me right under the walls of Alexandria, Octavian has surpassed my hopes and has fallen by his own hands in the trap which will take him? See where we are and decide whether Octavian or you has the better role? You, under the protection of these ramparts which brave all assault, with your legionnaires impatient for revenge and my army intact, and my granaries choking. He, pressed between a fortified city, hostile Egypt, an uncertain sea, and a threatening desert! Do you want to know what is needed this time for Egypt to devour Octavian and his army? Go to rest on your elbows on the ramparts for the sun to stand high over the deserts of Libya.
Then you will see with what whips my gods chase invaders!

ANTHONY
Are you counting on your gods?

CLEOPATRA
On the gods and on myself! Are your ships in the great harbor?

ANTHONY
Yes.

CLEOPATRA
Arrayed solidly, as I have given the order to Kephren and at a good distance from each other?

ANTHONY
Yes, why?

CLEOPATRA
We will see after the storm what remains of Octavian's camp and of his fleet!

ANTHONY
Storm? What do you mean? Your Diviner promises us the assistance of a storm?

CLEOPATRA
I promise it to you.

ANTHONY
With this blue heaven—

CLEOPATRA
Over our heads! But, already, towards Nubia, the horizon is drowning in vapors.

ANTHONY
It will be with us tonight?

CLEOPATRA
It will be with us in an instant! Do you forget with what speed the Typhon comes in the rainy season? See, my ibises have deserted the cornices, your hunting dogs, ordinarily so prompt to greet your return, have not yet greeted you with their baying. Listen, not the buzz of an insect, not the shivering of a leaf, not the cry of a bird! Nature, motionless, is silent, frozen by what's coming.

ANTHONY
Yes! One breathes fire.

CLEOPATRA
Let the hurricane loose, while we are in the shelter of the palace, our ships in the port, our soldiers in the caserne, let the black cavalry of waves fall on the camp of Octavian with thunder for drums, let them tear and disperse his tents, and let them clash and break his ships. At first light of dawn, you will throw yourself in your turn on his soldiers, weakened from a night of watchfulness and anxiety, and you will only have to choose between giving them for shrouds the sand of the desert or the whirlpools of the waves.

ANTHONY (struck)
Perhaps!

CLEOPATRA
And, you will triumph then, not in Rome, in Rome forever disillusioned by its defeat, but in my city, in the city of Alexandria—the heir and rival of Athens. Be great again, o my master, into the shape of my hero, joyous and strong in your image. Fill it with splendors and feasts. Open its doors to all the races of the Orient. Realize your dream of an Empire of the Sun, ruled by a couple of happy lovers. And make all the people of the earth forget the cursed name of Rome for that of my dear triumphant Alexandria.

ANTHONY
Yes! Perhaps! Yes, yes, if the storm rises as you say it will.

CLEOPATRA
In an instant! See these lotuses already fluttering from the surrounding air. When they bloom by themselves at the first breath of the Typhons, the light is ready to shine.

ANTHONY
And the storm fulfils its needs and ours. And the dawn will suffice for a vigorous sortie. By Pollux, Queen, you are right, always right! I am already shivering with impatience for combat and the presentiment of their defeat.

CLEOPATRA
And, if yet, fortune must betray us again, death will not.

ANTHONY
I knew, indeed, how to call it to me in battle.

CLEOPATRA
And, if Olympus' poison fails me, I will have, from tonight, one of those pretty Nile serpents whose poison gives a soft death.

ANTHONY (taking her passionately in his arms)
Swear it!

CLEOPATRA
I witness Isis, who hears me, that I will not survive you by an hour.

ANTHONY
Ah, terrible enchantment of my life, that I believed lost forever, that I retrieve with such drunken joy.

CLEOPATRA (in his arms)
Come, then, and this night again we will savor the sweetness of life.

KEPHREN (running in with sword in hand)
Alarm! Queen, look about you.

ANTHONY
What is it?

KEPHREN
The captains of your cohorts invade our gardens. They come, they say, by your order, for the sacrifice of the Queen that you promised them.

ANTHONY
I was forgetting.

CLEOPATRA (jokingly)
Ah, were we there?

Soldiers (outside)
Death! Death to the Egyptian.

KEPHREN
You hear them!

ANTHONY
The insolents.

CLEOPATRA
It's nothing. Tell the priests to come out of the temple with the images of our gods.

(Kephren goes to the temple. Enter Lictors, Demetrius, Dercetas, Juba, Roman Officers, People, then the Priests. The soldiers tumultuously invade the palace.)

SOLDIERS
Death to Cleopatra. Throw the Egyptian in the Nile! Glory to Mark Anthony. Judge! The sorceress to the Lictors, to the Lictors.

ANTHONY
Silence—and let none of you be so brave as to take another step.

(Surprise. They shut up, intimidated.)

DEMETRIUS
Mark Anthony, have you forgotten your words?

DERCETAS
Your oaths?

DEMETRIUS
It's by your order that we have controlled the centurions.

DERCETAS
And promised to all the sacrifice of this woman, which is their due.

(Soldiers press forward.)

SOLDIERS
Yes! Yes!

ANTHONY
Well, I have changed my opinion, that's all. (Astonishment.)

DEMETRIUS
Say that the sorceress has enchained you again.

DERCETAS
That she has made you drink some potion.

ANTHONY
Enough! Obey me and go.

(Dissatisfaction.)

DEMETRIUS
No. We won't obey.

ALL
No! No!

ANTHONY (threateningly)
You were saying?

DEMETRIUS
For you are no longer in your right mind.

DERCETAS
And, despite yourself, we will save you from yourself.

ANTHONY (furious)
You dare?

DEMETRIUS
Come on, friends!

ALL (drawing their swords)
Death to the Egyptian! To the sorceress! Down with the sorceress.

ANTHONY (jumping in front of Cleopatra)
Wretches! (drawing his sword)

CLEOPATRA
Stop! This is no longer your affair, but mine. (turns toward the soldiers and advances towards them) Yes, sorceress, yes magician! (soldiers recoil a step) Fools, who believe me in your power when you are in mine! And, thank the gods that it is so. For the sorceress only brought you within the walls of Alexandria to give you victory! (they look hesitant, surprised) And if, in an hour, Octavian and his army are only a memory, you will owe it to the enchantments of this magician.

DERCETAS (in a weak voice)
What is she saying?

DEMETRIUS
Is she making fun of us?

CLEOPATRA
On the African soil, all bow to my enchantments. The Typhon itself, the black god, the conqueror of Osiris! And, however far he may be, at the first call of my voice, his formidable voice will respond.

(Distant roll of thunder. The soldiers are intimidated, stupefied. Cleopatra alone with Anthony.)

CLEOPATRA
Typhon! Answer! Answer again. Witness that, for the love of Cleopatra, you are going to release on the enemy who besieges us, your whirlwinds and your thunder and that you will not give him quarter until he is mud, cinder or dust!

(New and rather prolonged rolls of thunder. All shiver.)

DEMETRIUS
O prodigy! The thunder obeys her like a dog its master.

(Music. Hymns. The procession of priests appear.)

CLEOPATRA
Cover your faces, rebels! Here are my gods and let none interrupt my invocations—unless he wishes to draw lightning on his head!

(The priests come out of the temple with statues of Osiris, Horus, and Isis, with harps and cymbals—and take up positions on the portico.)

CLEOPATRA
Typhon!

PRIESTS
Typhon.

ALL
Typhon!

CLEOPATRA
Typhon, king of the desert! Typhon, king of storms, whose feasts are disasters. Typhon who put the god of day at your knees. Hear Cleopatra! Hear us!

PRIESTS
Typhon, king of the desert! Typhon, king of storms.

CLEOPATRA
From the depths of burning Libya, where the lions hide like gazelles when the desert is full of whirlwinds, hurry with all the strength of your powerful winds. Come to us who supplicate you.

PRIESTS
Hurry with all the strength of your powerful winds. Come to us who supplicate you!

CLEOPATRA.
Come! The cloak of shadows is not enough. What lies on the sleeping waves, to these distant howls, to these funereal shouts, come, mix your roars.

(A light shines.)

PRIESTS
To these distant howls, to these funereal shouts, come mix your roars.

(Roll of distant thunder.)

CLEOPATRA
Closer! Again, o voice, strong and sublime, respond quickly to my voice.

(The thunder approaches.)

CLEOPATRA
Good! Again! And may all the echoes of the abyss shout at once.

PRIESTS
Again! Again, o voice, strong and sublime. Growl, bellow, thunder from your height in heaven, Typhon, devastator.

(The thunder increases. The lightning follows blindly.)

CLEOPATRA
Pierce them with arrows from your quiver full of lightning. Tear, scatter in the air his tents, thus like dry leaves.

PRIESTS
Disperse his vessels on the foam of the sea.

(The water spout breaks covered with rain.)

CLEOPATRA
Hurl them and strike them with madness. Soldiers at the feet of our towers, spoils of dogs and vultures.

PRIESTS
Grind them under your immense millstone.

(The lightning increases.)

CLEOPATRA
Hear them, hear them cry!

CLEOPATRA (then the priests)
Death is beneath their feet, Death is on their heads.

(All, Anthony, his lieutenants, Kephren and his archers, Olympus and the Soothsayer, mingle their shouts, prostrated before Cleopatra. A furious wind breaks through the palms.)

CLEOPATRA (then the Priests)
Erase them, Typhon, Strike good worker! Typhon, king of deserts, Typhon, king of storms, Wipe them out, the accursed. Strike, good worker.

(The storm breaks, formidable.

CURTAIN

ACT V

Scene 6

Alexandria

A hall in Cleopatra's palace, low and somber, covered with paintings. On the ceiling constellations, a series of symbols. In the background a bronze door with two panels. To the right and left two smaller doors, half masked by hangings. A bronze table in the middle and two armchairs of painted cedar wood.

It is still night. Charmian and Iris sleep on mats which frame the door by the right. The plume fans have fallen from their hands. Profound silence. Then some hurried steps outside. Someone knocks, at first discreetly, at the bronze door. Iris dresses.

IRIS
Charmian!

CHARMIAN (startled)
Huh? What is it?

IRIS (in a low voice)
Silence!

CHARMIAN (low)
What's happening?

IRIS
Don't you hear knocking?

CHARMIAN
No. At which door? That of the Queen?

(Charmian goes to the right.)

IRIS (going to the left)
It would rather be Kephren's. (knocking heard again) Listen! It's at the bronze door!

CHARMIAN
Already? It's hardly daybreak.

MAN (outside)
Iris.

IRIS
You see. (aloud) I am coming. (rises)

CHARMIAN
Don't open!

IRIS (near the door)
Who is it?

MAN
Aurosis. Open quickly.

IRIS (to Charmian)
It's Aurosis. The slave of Olympus.

CHARMIAN
You recognized his voice?

IRIS
Yes?

(She opens. Aurosis appears carrying a basket full of leaves.)

AUROSIS
Where is the Queen?

CHARMIAN
In her room.

AUROSIS
Wake her!

CHARMIAN
Do you dare? What have you got?

AUROSIS
What she asked from my master. (points to his basket)

CHARMIAN
Figs! Just for figs. (puts out her hand)

AUROSIS (excitedly)
Don't touch that and come here! Listen.

(Aurosis pulls Charmian to the doorway. Iris, curious, rises and goes to rejoin them.)

AUROSIS
Don't you understand?

(A moment of silence.)

CHARMIAN (listening)
Yes, all so far.

IRIS
Towards the east.

CHARMIAN
One would say a troop was marching.

AUROSIS
And, from that side, down there—towards the ramps of the palace, don't you see lights between the branches of the cypresses and sycamores?

IRIS
Yes, one would say scintillating water running toward the sun.

AUROSIS
From helmets! And from spear points.

CHARMIAN
Doubtless! They are making a sortie this morning. These are our soldiers who are going to take their positions while waiting the arrival of Anthony?

AUROSIS
Those are not our soldiers, Charmian, but Romans!

IRIS and CHARMIAN (terrified)
Holy Isis!

CHARMIAN
The storm has not annihilated them?

AUROSIS
It has made them more furious and in a greater hurry to finish things.

IRIS (running to the door at the right)
Misery! Kephren!

KEPHREN (outside)
Who calls me?

(Kephren enters hurriedly.)

IRIS and CHARMIAN (together, terrified)
The Romans! In the city!

KEPHREN
In the city? Are you losing your wits?

AUROSIS
I have seen them!

KEPHREN
You?

AUROSIS
With my own eyes while bringing the aspic the Queen asked for. I saw, I tell you, a group of Roman soldiers and officers, in a ship rushing toward the gate to the cisterns.

KEPHREN
Guarded by Thryseus!

AUROSIS
It was opened before them!

KEPHREN (frightened)
Treason!

AUROSIS
And, all still dripping from the rain of this storm, famished, covered with mud, but intrepid and sure of victory, the Roman army made its entry by this gate and silently circled the palace!

CHARMIAN and IRIS
By all the gods!

KEPHREN
All is lost! (to Iris and Charmian) The Queen! Quickly, awaken the Queen. (going toward the distance) Archers of the guard—to me! Where are the archers?

(Juba appears in the garden with several other officers of Anthony, hurrying from all sides, gesturing, frightened and pointing toward the town. At the moment Iris runs to Cleopatra's door, she herself enters.)

CLEOPATRA
What noise and what disturbances at my door! The hour to awaken the master has not come.

IRIS and CHARMIAN (choking, fluttering their hands)
Ah, Mistress.

CLEOPATRA (paying no attention to them, going to Aurosis)
Ah, it's you. (pointing to the basket) The serpent is there, right?

KEPHREN (returning, the others stay back)
They are everywhere! Queen, you are betrayed!

CLEOPATRA
Betrayed?

KEPHREN
By Thryseus, who has opened the gate of the cisterns to Octavian, by the mercenaries who opened the water gate to them; by your archers themselves, who have disappeared while Demetrius and Dercetas are at the ramparts where the assault is taking place.

CLEOPATRA (terrified)
Cruel gods! It is the end!

KEPHREN
Octavian's soldiers already hold the ramps of the palace. You can see them.

CLEOPATRA
Awaken Anthony and let him hasten to flee!

(Juba goes to the door at the right.)

KEPHREN
Impossible! The palace is surrounded on all sides!

CLEOPATRA (excitedly)
Then, don't wake him, then! He would fall on his sword or strangle himself. Ah, just gods. Revengeful gods. What can I do now to save him? What can be done!

KEPHREN
Strike down the victor.

CLEOPATRA
In the midst of his soldiers?

KEPHREN (drawing his cutlass)
I will, at least, attempt it.

CLEOPATRA (stopping him)
No! Not that way! Not down there! Here!

KEPHREN
So be it! How?

CLEOPATRA
Ah! I know him! How can I do it? My reason escapes me and the minutes rush on us. (raging) Still, it's indeed here that he must be killed, before he crosses the sill of this door. (points to the right) It

must be done! Help me! Search! Find a way. I cannot do it. I am going mad!

KEPHREN
I can be in hiding in my room.

CLEOPATRA
Yes, in your room! That's it! And, at the right moment. Ah, God, this is the last role to play! We cannot lose. In your room. Yes—and wait. Yes—that's it. (with joy) I've got it. (to Iris) Run to this monster, to Octavian!

IRIS (weeping, overwhelmed)
O, mistress, I—

CLEOPATRA (with strength)
Yes. Make him know you! Tell him—and don't refrain from crying, especially! Tell him that Cleopatra is here, in despair. That she sees herself already in Rome, hands tied before his chariot—and that I am only thinking of death. And that he must hasten if he wishes to find me still alive. He will come. I will answer for that. His only fear is not being able to have the Queen of Egypt to grace his triumph. Go. And cry, especially cry—cry more than you know how! (Iris goes out by the rear, to Kephren and Charmian) You, my faithful ones, listen well! I am going to arrange it so that Octavian and I will be alone here. (to Kephren) You, in your room, watching, ready to act without being seen. (to Charmian) You standing down there, near the door with Iris—not being uneasy. I will sit here—he will take the other armchair—and while I lull him with my words and draw his attention to me, (to Kephren) you will come up behind him on tip toe, and when you see me raise my fan like this (gesturing with a fan), you will take your cutlass and plunge the steel between his shoulders and strike him down like a bullock in an abattoir—with a single blow.

KEPHREN
Yes, Mistress.

CLEOPATRA (to CHARMIAN)
At the same signal, and quick as a flash, Iris, and you will shut the bronze door. We will run to Anthony's room. The rest is our affair. Octavian dead—all those who acclaim the act will acclaim us—and it's over. You have understood me?

KEPHREN and CHARMIAN
Yes, Mistress.

CLEOPATRA (making a gesture)
The fan—

KEPHREN
I strike

CHARMIAN
And we shut the door.

CLEOPATRA
And now—Kephren and you—hide. (Kephren disappears) May the gods aid us, for my well being and for yours. Here he is.

(Octavian appears in the doorway at back, accompanied by Thryseus. Behind him, a group of Roman officers. Iris precedes him, showing the way.)

OCTAVIAN (after having taken a single step across the doorway, to Iris)
The Queen of Egypt is here, you say?

(Iris points to Cleopatra, standing motionless.)

THRYSEUS
Yes, Master, here is Cleopatra.

(Octavian slowly advances.)

OCTAVIAN (whispers to Thryseus)
She is truly beautiful.

THRYSEUS (low)
Take care.

OCTAVIAN (smiling)
Fine! I am neither Caesar nor Mark Anthony. (to Cleopatra, still motionless) Queen—for you are still Queen—

CLEOPATRA (to herself)
Hypocrite!

OCTAVIAN
This woman made me fear that, from despair and fright, you would attempt your life. I am here to assure you, that from me, personally, you have nothing to fear.

CLEOPATRA
Then, Caesar, deign to give me a first proof of your good will by not forcing me to blush before these men, who are only too happy to contemplate the humiliation of a Queen, and consent to speak to you here—face to face—if you are not, like the others, afraid of Cleopatra.

(Octavian consults Thryseus with a look.)

THRYSEUS (low)
There's no danger!

OCTAVIAN
So be it! (to his officers) Leave us! (returning) But, don't go far off. (to Thryseus, low) You, now—finish! You know the palace?

THRYSEUS (low)
As Anthony himself.

OCTAVIAN
Go, while I amuse her with some pleasant words.

THRYSEUS
Living, also?

OCTAVIAN
Or dead!

THRYSEUS
Better!

(He leaves and joins with a group of armed men. One can see officers in the distance going to and fro on the terrace, two by two, in discussion. During the preceding dialogue Cleopatra has spoken to Charmian and Iris who prepare the chairs and go nonchalantly to the door, standing easily on each side of it, motionless—never losing sight of their mistress.)

CLEOPATRA (standing)
Caesar, the gods have given you victory, and now that we are alone, I can, without confusion, greet you as the master of my fate. Don't leave me for a long time in this cruel anxiety. What have you decided about me?

OCTAVIAN (also standing)
Nothing as yet! For the moment, I am pleasantly contemplating that which has made such a noise in the world, and the more I look at her, the more Mark Anthony seems excusable to me.

CLEOPATRA (bitterly)
You are joking?

OCTAVIAN
Preserve me from it, gods! But (signals her to sit), as regards Anthony—(Cleopatra sits at the armchair near the table)—why haven't

I seen him? Has he given up defending you? I didn't think he was ungrateful to such a degree.

(He comes to the table, standing. Kephren is approaching, hidden by the tapestries. The coming and going of the officers on the terrace unnerves Cleopatra.)

CLEOPATRA
Anthony left the city before dawn. (watching the officers on the terrace) To Memphis—where he is counting on rallying an Army of Upper Egypt.

OCTAVIAN
You gave him that advice?

CLEOPATRA
Yes.

OCTAVIAN (hand in the back of the armchair at the left)
And, why didn't you accompany him in his flight?

CLEOPATRA
He himself opposed it, in the hope that my submission would disarm your rage and that your grace would grant me life.

OCTAVIAN
It would be wrong, let us agree, to destroy such a perfect example of feminine beauty.

(He sits in the armchair. Gesture of satisfaction by Cleopatra. Kephren closes in. In the distance, a group of officers stops.)

CLEOPATRA
Enough of my life. Let us speak of my throne. A Queen cannot, without dishonor, ask for less than a kingdom. Will you leave me mine?

OCTAVIAN
That's a question to which only Rome can give an answer.

CLEOPATRA (with a dolorous sigh, feigning a faint)
Then, his reply was foreseen. It's my dethronement.

(Furtively Cleopatra watches the officers outside without being seen by Octavian. The officers continually come and go.)

CLEOPATRA
I will be free, at least.

OCTAVIAN
I hope so.

CLEOPATRA (insistently)
But, without being sure of it?

OCTAVIAN
Rome—
(Cleopatra goes toward the table to attract Octavian's attention and facilitate Kephren's approach.)

CLEOPATRA
Always Rome! Your generosity assures me, at least, that you will not condemn me to the horror of adorning your triumph and walking with naked feet before your chariot, under sneers of the Roman mob. If you require it, for my ransom, I will abandon all my treasures.

OCTAVIAN (jokingly)
You are forgetting that your treasures are—from today—mine.

(Now the officers depart. Kephren moves closer to Octavian.)

CLEOPATRA
Then, let pity be my sole ransom! In the name of the gods who are prompt to punish those without pity, in the name of your adoptive father Caesar, who loved me, and of whom you are the living image.

OCTAVIAN
I will consult the Senate.

CLEOPATRA (reaching for her fan)
Then—

(Kephren raises his cutlass. Suddenly furious cries from behind the door at right. The noise of a struggle dominated by Anthony's voice.)

ANTHONY (outside)
Ah, wretches! Rogues!

(Octavian rises and quickly goes to the terrace, avoiding Kephren without, in fact, seeing him. Kephren can no longer attack Octavian. Octavian's officers run up, attracted by the noise and place him beyond all danger.

CLEOPATRA (standing, ashen pale)
That voice. Those shouts.

KEPHREN
That of the master.

CLEOPATRA
They are strangling him! (runs to the door) Assassins! Assassins! (pointing out Octavian to Kephren) But, kill this one, then. Kill him.

(The officers step forward, protecting Octavian.)

ANTHONY (outside)
To me, Kephren!

CLEOPATRA (running to open the door)
Courage, we are here. Hold on! (Kephren runs to the door; Cleopatra tries to force it open) Ah, wretches!

KEPHREN (breaking down the door)
That's done.

ANTHONY
Too late.

(He enters with Eros, staggering, wounded, a broken sword in his hand and falls into the arms of Cleopatra. The murderers rush by Kephren and disappear. Kephren pushes the door shut and returns to Anthony.)

CLEOPATRA
Wounded! Yes, some blood. Wounded. Ah, gods!

ANTHONY (breathing heavily)
In my sleep—the cowards! (perceiving Octavian, who is watching him) This is worthy of you, bandit. (pulling himself from the arms of Cleopatra and taking a threatening step towards Octavian, who recoils instinctively) See him, the coward. (roaring with laughter) Dying as I am, I can still scare you!

OCTAVIAN (calmly)
The vanquished have a right to insult. Let him end in peace. (mechanically to Anthony) I forgive him everything, on the condition that he dies!

(He leaves at the back, followed by Thryseus and his officers. Kephren shuts the door on him.)

CLEOPATRA (on her knees, near Anthony)
That he dies! Holy Isis! Is it come to that? Save him! (to Kephren) Olympus, help me. These cushions— (Kephren departs left while

the women bring the cushions.) Anthony, my Anthony, do you hear me?

ANTHONY (troubled, gasping)
Yes, still. I hear your voice. But, I can hardly see you. Where are you, my love?

CLEOPATRA (weeping)
Here, in your arms.

ANTHONY (taking her hand)
Come, very near, that I may see your adored eyes.

CLEOPATRA
Oh, my beloved.

ANTHONY
Yes, they are here. But, why full of tears? Did we not resolve to die? I am fallen, sword in hand, as a soldier. I die worthy of my name, and people to come will envy me, since I die in your arms.

CLEOPATRA
No, no! You shall not die! Olympus! Olympus doesn't come. (to Eros) Child, run to the temple in the palace and tell the priests to implore our gods.

(Eros runs out left.)

ANTHONY
What's the use? Doctors and priests can do nothing. Already my soul beats its wings. My long journey is finished. It's the evening of the battle—let us sleep, yet one more kiss! After so many kisses, my beloved, yet one more—the last.

CLEOPATRA
Wait! Oh, wait. Don't leave me so soon. Charmian!

(Cleopatra points to the basket, Charmian hesitates.)

CLEOPATRA (to Anthony)
We will go together. We are married, you know it. Wait for me.

ANTHONY (dying)
What are you going to do?

CLEOPATRA
Follow you!

ANTHONY
Hasten. Your hand. Your lips, again. Come, quickly. (He dies sweetly in her arms. Song of the priests in the distance are heard until the fall of the curtain.)

CLEOPATRA (softly placing Anthony on the cushion)
It's over. And, this adored mouth has spoken to me for the last time. (kisses his lips) Come! Cleopatra, in your turn.

(She opens the basket.)

CHARMIAN and IRIS (in tears, imploring her on their knees.
Oh? Mistress!

CLEOPATRA
Be quiet, Charmian! Courage, Iris! (separating the leaves and finding the snake) And you, pretty reptile, wake up! (She takes the snake and agitates it! Come, attach yourself here like a child to the breast of his mother. (places it in her arms, her teeth tight together, closing her eyes.

(Charmian is crying on her knees)

IRIS (also weeping)
Flower of beauty.

CLEOPATRA (in a firmer voice)
Come! No tears! You heard him. Mark Anthony doesn't want tears. Again, sweet little beast Again. (drops the snake) Here you see me, my Anthony, do Romans die more gracefully? (To Charmian) Give me my mirror, so I can see if I remain beautiful? (looks at herself and smiles) I think I do. Thanks. Put my crown on my head and my scepter in my hand. And, in Anthony's hand, his sword. (watches them cry) Poor girls, what will become of you without me?

CHARMIAN (to herself)
We won't leave you—even in death.

CLEOPATRA
I am going to sleep, I feel it, rocked by waves. By waves, under a clear sun. I am on the Cydnus—and I am going to meet Anthony. Are you there, Charmian?

CHARMIAN
Yes, Queen.

CLEOPATRA
Open the door. The valiant Octavian has nothing more to fear. Anthony is dead! Who calls me? You, my hero? Patience, I am here. I am coming, my Royal Lord. Patience, I am coming.

(Cleopatra dies, smiling.)

CURTAIN

ABOUT FRANK J. MORLOCK

FRANK J. MORLOCK has written and translated many plays since retiring from the legal profession in 1992. His translations have also appeared on Project Gutenberg, the Alexandre Dumas Père web page, Literature in the Age of Napoléon, Infinite Artistries.com, and Munsey's (formerly Blackmask). In 2006 he received an award from the North American Jules Verne Society for his translations of Verne's plays. He lives and works in México.

www.ingramcontent.com/pod-product-compliance
Lightning Source LLC
LaVergne TN
LVHW041620070426
835507LV00008B/354